GOD
IN THE
WORLD

Christianity and Judaism — The Formative Categories

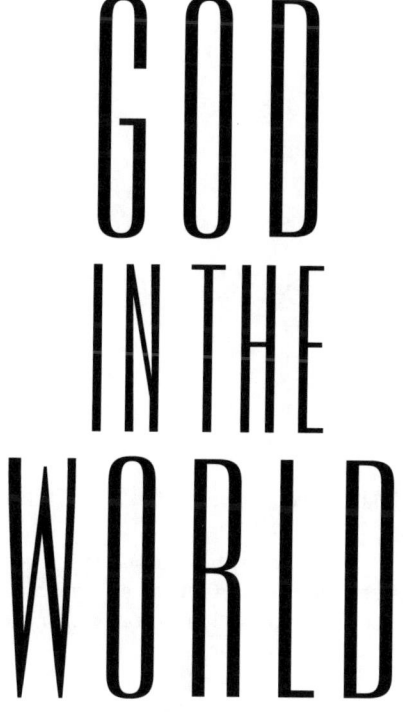

GOD
IN THE
WORLD

Jacob Neusner
Bruce D. Chilton

TRINITY PRESS INTERNATIONAL
Harrisburg, Pennsylvania

Trinity Press International, P.O. Box 1321, Harrisburg, PA 17105
Trinity Press International is a division of the Morehouse Group

Library of Congress Cataloging-in-Publication Data

Neusner, Jacob, 1932-
  God in the world / Jacob Neusner, Bruce D. Chilton.
    p.   cm. – (Christianity and Judaism, the formative
  categories)
    Includes bibliographical references and index.
    ISBN 1-56338-202-4 (alk. paper)
    1. God (Judaism) – Knowableness. 2. Jesus Christ – Intercession.
  3. Incarnation.   I. Chilton, Bruce. II. Title. III. Series.
  Neusner, Jacob, 1932-   Christianity and Judaism, the formative
  categories.
  BM610.N47 1997
  296.3'117–dc21   97-35414
                                                                        CIP

Printed in the United States of America

97 98 99 00 01   10 9 8 7 6 5 4 3 2 1

Contents

Preface

Christianity and Judaism, along with Islam, by their own testimony seek to reach the same God, but each takes its own path. In common, all three invoke the same authority, Abraham and Sarah, represented by the same Scriptures, and all three worship the one and only God, concurring that the God of which each speaks is the same God that the others adore. At the same time, each distinguishes itself from the other two, finding important differences at specific points and maintaining that it, and not the others, accurately records what that one, unique God has said. Sustained argument can take place when people who agree on premises and principles also disagree on propositions and conclusions, and Judaism, Islam, and Christianity can sustain, and for determinate periods in the past did mount, a cogent and illuminating argument.

Among the three, because of the intimacy of their contacts — historical and geographical alike — Judaism and Christianity have formed the closest relationship, which, in the very recent past, has turned cordial. Aforetimes, the relationship was one of contempt and incomprehension, each for the absurdities of the other. Imputations of guilt, recriminations, not to mention exclusion and even murder, ruined any possibilities for mutual illumination of self-respecting and honored partners in dialogue. Now, for the first time, in the United States and in the English-speaking world in general, differences between those two complex sets of religious traditions come under discussion free of rancor and recrimination. Consequently, outlining the points of concurrence and those of conflict may take place in a spirit of enlightenment and friendship, not to negotiate, or even place limits upon, difference, but only to understand the other more fully and more accurately.

Our purpose here is to compare and contrast the paramount theological categories of Judaism and Christianity, each meaning to inform the other of the main points of the classical theology of his religious tradition on matters of concern to the other. Each, moreover, takes a position at the end of the exposition accomplished by the other, taking seriously and commenting upon points of likeness and difference in the account set forth by the other. So we mean to describe, then compare and contrast, the main theological structures on which our respective faiths are constructed.

We do not propose to obscure theological difference, nor to sidestep profound disagreement in quest of a socially useful goal of amity. On the contrary, we seek a different goal from theological negotiation; neither is "liberal" about his own beliefs, let alone "tolerant" of the choices made by the other. Each believes in his tradition and its affirmations, and each without apology or excuse practices that tradition. Neither proposes to permit long-term friendship and partnership in intellectual projects to impose conditions on the integrity of his faith, nor wants the other to. Both of us are educators and scholars, firm in the conviction that knowledge and understanding affirm our convictions but also willing to yield respect for differing ones. We each seek to grasp the rationality of the views of the other, in full awareness that it is a different rationality.

In these three volumes, we propose to provide the faithful of both Judaism and Christianity with an informative, factual account of how, in their classical formulations, Christianity and Judaism addressed the same issues and set forth each its own distinctive program and set of propositions. This is plausible and productive for several reasons.

First, we have lived side by side for nearly two thousand years; each knows a great deal about the other. We have been neighbors for a long time, and now we are striving to become friends. Neither proposes to surrender the slightest point of distinctiveness, and both affirm the ultimate difference of the one from the other. But since all parties concur that we really do worship the same God and we differ about how we know that same God and what that God has made manifest to us, the possibility of educating ourselves about the other emerges: we disagree about the same things. And we also agree about much.

Second, because Christianity and Judaism in structure and even system are so much alike, it is possible to compare their theological views of the same questions. Because they so vigorously disagree on the main points, it also is interesting to do so. We do not mean, here, to carry forward the centuries' old disputations between the two great religious traditions of the West but to use each to illuminate the other.

Third, because Christianity and Judaism (along with Islam) today confront as partners the challenges of militant secularism and proselytizing atheism, we find ourselves drawn together to address a common enemy. From the late eighteenth century to nearly our own day, practitioners of Judaism stood by while ethnic Jews allied the Jewish population with militant secularism. Nearly all Jews, including practitioners of Judaism ("Judaists"), took for granted, and with ample cause, that only in a neutral, secular society could Jews survive as a distinct group and could Judaism be practiced. Communal secularism within Jewry moreover held together the religious sector of the community, the Judaists, and the secular sector, the solely ethnic Jews. Only in the most recent past has a different perspective on the imperatives of the public square reshaped vision; now a growing minority within the Jewish community find their friends outside not in militant secularism but in Christians of good will, Roman Catholic and Protestant and Orthodox. With them Judaists make common cause in a number of shared projects, even while carefully agreeing to set aside all theological discourse. The Judaic partner in these books concurs with this minority view. Judaists and Christians, loyal to their respective faiths, recognize urgent, shared commitments to the social order.

Now it is that very new, but very promising, recognition of mutuality of interest that calls for precisely the kind of book that the two authors of these volumes mean to write together. For mutuality of interest depends in the end upon mutuality of understanding. By that we mean that we simply have to get to know one another better than we now do. For shared labors for the public interest are best carried out by people who, agreeing to disagree on some things and to work together on others, deeply respect and fully understand the difference that separates them. And that requires knowledge, not the pretense that some subjects lie beyond all discourse. Precisely what the body of Christ means to the Christian, or the election of Israel (the holy people) to the Judaist, what the Torah tells the Judaist and the Bible the Christian, how God is made manifest in this world, that is, is "incarnate," to both Judaist and Christian — these fundamental points of commonality in structure and conflict in system require exposition, and it is that exposition that we promise in these books.

Ours is not a relationship of sentimentality or careful avoidance of difference. We do not believe that, at the foundations, we really are the same, and neither wants to become like the other or to give up any part of what makes him different from the other in the most profound layers of conviction and calling. The one writer is called to the study of the Torah as his way of life and purpose of being; the other is called to follow God's wisdom and power as his only Son has revealed them. But for the one the study of the Torah and for the other the wisdom of Christ carry learning beyond the boundaries of the Torah and of Christ, respectively. Each finds his work possible only through learning more about the religion of the other. And both maintain that sound learning and authentic understanding of their respective faiths demand attention to the near-at-hand religion of the other.

Still, we work together in a personal, though not a theological, partnership. Not only are the two authors long-time friends, but we come in an irenic spirit, genuinely fond of one another and also respectful of the call that each acknowledges God has vouchsafed to the other. We cannot explain how God has spoken in such different terms to so many people. We do not know why God has made us so different from one another — all the while seeking to serve that one and the same true God. But we know that, within the traditions that shape our lives and minds, we are constrained to recognize that the other is possessed of the same revelation that we revere. Since the Judaic partner understands that Christianity's "Old Testament" is his "written Torah," and since the Christian partner recognizes the same fact, both share the common ground that here God has said the same thing to each, and, on that account comparison and contrast become options, ones we now wish to explore. Firm in our convictions, neither of us asks the other to surrender his beliefs; we are not going to say which of us, from God's viewpoint, is right. In the fullness of time, God will not only decide, but make the decision known. For the interim, we accept the situation of indeterminacy: each of us is sure he is right, but neither finds the other's assent — therefore, conversion — a condition of mutual education. There is a very practical reason for that shared decision, even while for the two of us it also represents a dimension of religious conviction to leave for God the final choice.

If we do not choose here to debate who is right, it is in some part because through long centuries that debate has gone on, and we doubt much is left to be said. Nor has the debate proved very illuminating or productive when framed in terms of truth and error. But we do wish to provide for faithful believers in Judaism and Christianity a systematic and fair-minded picture of what both religions say about the same things. The differences coincide: Torah or Bible, Israel or Church, the media of God's this-worldly incarnation. In our view, religious dialogue, including debate, benefits us all. Our theory — and here we speak only for ourselves personally and not for the Church or the Torah — is that each has learned something about God that the other must want to know, even while each of us knows full well that the criterion of truth rests, as it has always rested, with, for Judaism, the Torah, and, for Christianity, Christ. But that up-front affirmation of difference defines not the end, but only the beginning, of the dialogue that we believe in the end serves the greater glory of the one God who has been made manifest to us all, not only in different ways, but, through Scripture, in one and the same way too.

For we both value "the Book," that is, the Hebrew Scriptures of ancient Israel. What that means should be made clear, since the issues that divide us are theological and not exegetical. Many hold that because both Judaism and Christianity share the same Scriptures — the written Torah, the Old Testament, being mostly concentric — the debate between them concerns the meaning of those writings. We take a different view. What we share, and that concerning which we differ, is not how to read the received and revealed Scriptures, but what we know about God, which to be sure is founded in those Scriptures. But knowledge of God derives from theology, not from literary criticism or the exegesis of sources.

That is why we frame our comparisons in theological terms — God, the body of faith, the presence of God in the world — rather than in the contrasts between one party's reading of pertinent verses of Scripture and the other party's reading of those same verses. The reason is that theology does not recapitulate Scripture, but the exegesis of Scripture recapitulates theology; and the further reason is that in any event for neither party is the Scripture of ancient Israel the sole and complete account of God's revelation to humanity. For Christianity the New Testament and for Judaism the oral part of the Torah are required; so the issue is not exegetical at all. It concerns how we fill with meaning the shared and common generative categories of the theological structure on which both build their systems: God, Torah, Israel, for Judaism; God, Christ, Church, for Christianity.

We underline, therefore, that for each of us Israelite Scripture, though held in common, is contingent, because each of us complements the shared Scriptures with further revelation. Judaism knows those Scriptures as the written part, which along with the oral part comprises the one whole Torah that God gave ("revealed") to Moses, our rabbi, at Mount Sinai. Christianity knows those same Scriptures as the Old Testament, which, along with the New Testament, comprises the Bible, the word of God. Because of the rich heritage of Scripture, with its ethics and morality and its account of what God wants of humanity, who God is, and what we are, many have concluded that a unitary "Judaeo-Christian tradition" defines the common religion of the West; Judaism and Christianity then are supposed to differ on details but concur on the main points. The opposite is the fact, and here we propose a different reading of the relationship between the two heirs of ancient Israel in the West.

Specifically, we spell out how, because they concur on so

much, the two religious traditions, Judaism and Christianity, differ in a very explicit and precise way. They talk about the same things, they invoke the same evidence, they rest their respective cases on the same premises of thought and rules of argument. And they profoundly differ. They are religions that divide on precisely what unites them, and their shared agenda of faith in and love for God accounts for the vigor and precision of their disagreements. That is to say, Judaism and Christianity identify in common the same principal and generative categories for the formulation of the religious life: revelation, social order, and the encounter with God. In Judaism, these categories bear the titles "Torah," "Israel," and, of course, "God in this world," which, in the classical documents of formative Judaism, encompasses diverse ways in which, in the here and now, we meet God. In Christianity, the counterparts are "the Bible," "the Church," and "Christ Incarnate."

In these three volumes, therefore, we identify and spell out in an elementary way the three principal areas of communion among, and therefore conflict between, the heirs of the same Scripture:

1. how and what we know about God, that is, the character of revelation;

2. who constitutes the people to whom God is made manifest, that is, the definition of the body of the faithful; and

3. where and through whom we meet God in this world.

Each religious tradition sets forth its definition of revelation; each defines the social order to whom God has spoken and has called into being in God's service; and of course each knows where and how, in this world, we meet God in human encounter.

We focus on the classical and definitive documents of the two traditions. In Judaism that is, for revelation, the Torah as it took shape in the first six centuries of the Common Era; the account of who and what "Israel" is in those same writings; the exposition of ways in which, in everyday life, God enters into the situation of ordinary people: how we meet God this morning, right here, as those documents portray the encounter. For Christianity, the counterpart literature is the New Testament, especially the Gospels. The first three Gospels constitute an introduction to the meaning of baptism, a life of solidarity with Christ. The correspondence among communities of Christians (above all, the letters of Paul) reflects the place of controversy in the life of faith. Finally, the Gospel of John, as well as works such as Colossians, Ephesians, and Hebrews, represent the great synthesis which made the emergence of a coherent Christianity possible. Both authors elect to limit discussion to the classical writings in the clear recognition that both religions unfolded through time, so that later writers expanded and recast the classical definitions and even categories. But we maintain that, however things changed, through time, the classical formulation remains the paramount one.

We mean to speak to Jews and Christians who want better to understand their own religious traditions. In our view, when we identify the issues that theological teachings address and understand the alternative positions on those issues that classical thinkers have adopted for themselves, we treat religion as vital. We cease to regard as self-evident the views we hold, but grasp that they represent decisions among options, choices people have made in full consideration of alternatives. Then our respective religions take on weight and consequence and become living choices among alternative truths. Only by seeing the options that have faced the framers of Judaism and Christianity in their classical writings shall we understand how, in full rationality and with entire awareness of issues and options, the founders of our respective traditions took the paths that they did. When religion is reduced to platitudes and banalities, lifelessly repeating things deemed to be self-evident, it loses all consequence and forms a mere chapter in the conventions of culture. But from Judaism and Christianity, for centuries stretching far into the past, faithful Israel, on the one side, and the living body of Christ, on the other, drew sustenance and found the strength to endure.

Let us not at the end lose sight of the remarkable power of these religions in times past and in our own day. The world did not make life easy for Judaism through its history in the West, and in the age of militant secularism, on the one side, and violently anti-Christian Communism, on the other, Christianity has found itself back in the catacombs. The century that now closes has afforded to the faith of Israel and of Christ no honor, and to the Israelite and to the Christian no respect by reason of loyalty to that vocation. Christianity outlived Communism in the USSR and its colonies. At the sacrifice of home and property, even at the price of life itself, Israel resisted the world's corrosive insistence that Israel cease to exist, but has reaffirmed its eternal calling. For whatever the choice of private persons, that social order formed by Israel on the one side, and the Church of Jesus Christ, on the other, has endured, against it all, despite it all, through all time and change. The act of defiance of fate in the certainty of faith in God's ultimate act of grace is the one thing God cannot have commanded, but it is what, in times of terrible stress, Judaic and Christian faithful have given freely and of their own volition. God can have said, and did say, "Serve me," but God could only beseech, "and trust me too."

For even God cannot coerce trust. Only Israel, only the Church could give what God could only ask, but not compel: the gifts of the heart, love and trust, for which the loving God yearns, which only the much-loved Israel or those who have been called into the churchly community can yield freely, of their own volition. And that is what Israel, in response to Sinai, and Christendom, in response to the empty tomb, willingly gave, and by their loyal persistence freely give today. These facts of human devotion tell us the power of the faiths that in these pages meet for a theological comparison. The stakes then are very high indeed.

•

We call attention to our complementary project, *Judaeo-Christian Debates: Communion with God, the Kingdom of God, the Mystery of the Messiah* (Minneapolis: Fortress Press, 1998). The two projects are readily distinguished. In this one, we compare and contrast the principal components of the counterpart structures of Judaism and Christianity, and in the other, we do the same for the counterpart systems of the two traditions. Here, in these three volumes, we spell out how the two faiths compare when set forth side by side; in the companion work, we explain how they function in comparable, sometimes parallel, ways: how each brings about communion with God, how each defines the worldly life of the faithful under God's dominion, and how each addresses the issue of teleology through the medium of eschatology. We express our thanks to the publishers of both projects for their willingness to let us do the work in the way that we have devised.

The joint authors express their thanks to Bard College and the University of South Florida for ongoing support for their scholarly work. Each author has found for himself ideal conditions for a life of learning, and neither takes for granted the gifts that he receives in these centers of higher learning. Both express thanks, also, to Dr. Harold Rast, publisher of Trinity Press International, for his commitment to this project and his guidance in bringing it to fruition. If we achieve our goal of a sustained theological encounter of an illuminating character, it is because of his guidance and long-term commitment to this project of ours.

BRUCE CHILTON
Bard College

JACOB NEUSNER
*University of South Florida
and Bard College*

Introduction

Incarnation in Judaism and Christianity: How God Is Made Manifest in the World

"So God created man in his own image, in the image of God he created him; male and female he created them."

Gen. 1:27

Heirs to the common Scripture of ancient Israel, both Judaism and Christianity identify humanity as the worldly image of God. No religions in humanity have ever offered to humanity a higher conception of what it means to be human. Judaism and Christianity concur, moreover, that, since we are made in God's image, in the face of one another we see God. The conception of incarnation is as Judaic as it is Christian. The point of difference between the two becomes clear when we ask precisely how incarnation is realized. These two accounts of the matter serve as an introduction to the detailed answer to that question set forth in this book.

Incarnation in Judaism: God Made Manifest in the Torah

The Torah has revealed, and through sages' learning in discipleship to Moses, our rabbi, continues to reveal, whatever it is about God that humanity is going to know. Therefore it is the

1

task of humanity to study the Torah in order to strive to imitate God, and that means to conform to the ways of God as the Torah defines those ways. Accordingly, as we follow the unfolding of the representation of God through the successive documents of the oral Torah, we trace the Judaic account of what it means to be "in our image, after our likeness."

Israel knows God through the Torah, which reports to Israel exactly what God has told and what sages have handed on from the revelation at Sinai. Our rapid survey of the oral Torah's reading of the written Torah allows us to follow the unfolding of the doctrine of God in classical Judaism.

Through the Torah, Judaism claims to afford knowledge of God through God's own self-manifestation. In the nature of things, that means self-manifestation to this world and in this world; for the sages of Judaism, knowledge of God concerned how we know God in the here and now; incarnation was a very familiar conception to them, since the received Scriptures everywhere portrayed God in terms of feelings, attitudes, emotions, and other attributes that were consubstantial with those of human beings. God was represented both as "holy other" but also as passionately engaged with Israel's everyday life: furious or ardent, as the occasion required. Emotions and attitudes form qualities of incarnation as much as physical attributes do, but, as a matter of fact, in Scripture and in the oral part of the Torah as well, God is given physical qualities as much as emotional and intellectual ones.

The Torah then claims to mediate God's self-manifestation, and the Torah promises to inform in two senses of the term: to illuminate, but also to reshape. The mind is informed, given truth it otherwise cannot gain; it is informed, given the power of analysis and argument to gain truth it otherwise cannot gain. Defining and shaping intellect in particular, "Judaism" or "the Torah" inform by forming human intellect in the model of God's intellect. Theology concerns the knowledge of God that, in accord with the view of a given religion, God affords to us. In the case of Judaism all the knowledge of God that Judaism alleges God has given to humanity is contained in the Torah. That is what theology proposes to describe and explain: the rational principles that govern knowledge in general applied to knowledge of God through the designated source in particular.

So theology simply is not to be confused with either philosophy, the sources of which are not revealed truth but demonstrated facts, or sociology, which in the study of religion tells us what people think they know about God and how they conduct themselves on that account. In Judaism the task of theology is to form an account of what we know about God in this world, what it means to know God in the framework of human knowledge and understanding. It is in that dimension that the Torah's account of God in this world is to be understood.

To understand the way in which Judaism in its classical documents sets forth how we know God in this world, we have to understand the unfolding of that Judaism. The Judaism (or Judaic system) of the dual Torah, which through time became normative, took shape in the progression from its beginning as philosophy through its transformation into religion and onward to its re-presentation as theology. That Judaic system presented an account of the way of life and worldview that a social entity called "Israel" formulated in response to the Pentateuch. Seen whole, its statement was set forth by the written Torah and also by the first written version of (part of) the oral component of the Torah, which was the Mishnah (ca. 200 C.E.). That document made its systemic statement in philosophical categories.

The framing of the statement of the Torah was then transformed into other, religious categories. This was by the categorical reformulation (the formation of counterpart categories) accomplished in the Talmud of the Land of Israel (ca. 400 C.E.) and its associated Midrash compilations, the earlier ones represented by Sifra and one of the Sifrés, the later by Leviticus Rabbah. The same Judaic system was finally restated as theology by the final document to contain in written form the oral component of the Torah, which was the Talmud of Babylonia, or Bavli (ca. 600 C.E.), and its companion Midrash collections, exemplified by Song of Songs Rabbah, Ruth Rabbah, and Lamentations Rabbati.

For the framers of the Bavli, what it means to be "in our image, after our likeness," is not only to act like God ("You shall be holy as I the Lord your God am holy· just as I am merciful and long-suffering, so must you be merciful and long-suffering"; "You shall be holy, for I the Lord your God am holy," that is to say, "if you sanctify yourselves, I shall credit it to you as though you had sanctified me, and if you do not sanctify yourselves, I shall hold that it is as if you have not sanctified me" (Sifra 195:1.3A–B]). To be "in our image" is also to think in full consciousness, in accord with articulated rules of rationality, like God. The Torah teaches how God speaks, and therefore how God thinks — but it is only in the Talmud that we find a sustained and articulated effort to show in detail the meaning of that how.

Much stress in the oral part of the Torah is laid on attitudes, feelings, and emotions: both God's and humanity's. The sages' notion of the centrality of human feelings in the religious life presents no surprises. Scripture is explicit on both sides of the matter. The human being is commanded to love God. God's emotional life is likewise registered. In the biblical biography of God, the tragic hero, God, will despair, love, hope, feel disappointment or exultation. The biblical record of God's feelings and God's will concerning the feelings of humanity — wanting human love, for example — leaves no room for doubt. Nor does Judaism ignore the datum that "the merciful God wants the heart." The rabbis of the Torah make explicit that God always wants the heart. God commands that humanity love God with full heart, soul, mind, and might. That is the principal duty of humanity. But the sages' contribution, from the Mishnah forward, proves distinctive and definitive.

In writings redacted in the earlier stages in the formation of the Judaism of the dual Torah, beginning with the Mishnah, God does not make an appearance as a vital personality, with whom other personalities — human ones — transact affairs. Other documents, in particular in the later stages in the unfolding of that same canonical system, by contrast, represent God in quite personal terms. These are three: outer traits, inner characteristics, and capacity for concrete action done as human beings carry out their wishes. That is to say, in some of these later documents God appears in corporeal form. God exhibits traits of emotion and exemplifies virtuous attitudes. God carries out actions as human beings do — and does them in the same way. That is the portrait of God appearing as a personality, not as a mere premise of being, abstract presence, or even disembodied person.

Let us spell out the substantive stages in the unfolding of God in Judaism's formative documents. In the first of the documents that make up the oral part of the Torah, which is the Mishnah, we speak of what Israel knows about God. But in later compilations, Israel no longer knows only about God. God then is set forth as more than a principle and a premise of being (in the way that philosophers understand God) and more, even, than as a presence (in the way that pious people know about God through prayer). Rather, Israel knows God as a person and, at the end of the formation of the oral Torah, even as a fully embodied personality. Sages know God in four aspects:

1. principle or premise, that is, the one who created the world and gave the Torah;

2. presence, e.g., supernatural being resident in the Temple and present where two or more persons engaged in discourse concerning the Torah;

3. person, e.g., the one to whom prayer is addressed; and

4. personality, a God we can know and make our model.

In the oral Torah, then, we find God portrayed in the earlier writings, as (1) premise and (2) presence, and in later writings also as (3) person, and finally, in the last phase of the formation of the oral Torah, the Talmud of Babylonia, as (4) personality. Let us consider these four dimensions of God, the measure by which we grasp the character of divinity in the Judaism under study. These dimensions are concrete and specific; we can readily determine where and when and how we may take the measure dictated by each of them.

1. God as premise occurs in passages in which an authorship reaches a particular decision because that authorship believes God created the world and has revealed the Torah to Israel. We therefore know that God forms the premise of a passage because the particular proposition of that passage appeals to God as premise of all being, e.g., author and authority of the Torah.

Things are decided one way rather than some other on that basis. That conviction of the givenness of God who created the world and gave the Torah self-evidently defines the premise of all Judaisms before our own times. There is nothing surprising in it. But a particular indicator in so general a fact derives from the cases in which for concrete and specific reasons sages invoke God as foundation and premise of the world. When do they decide a case or reach a decision because they appeal to God as premise, and when do they not do so? But this conception is much more subtle, since the entire foundation of the Mishnah, the initial statement of the oral Torah, rests upon the conception of the unity of God. The purpose of the Mishnah is to show how, in the here and now of the social and natural world, we see what it means that God is one.

2. God as presence stands for yet another consideration. It involves an authorship's referring to God as part of a situation in the here and now. When an authorship — e.g., of the Mishnah — speaks of an ox goring another ox, it does not appeal to God to reach a decision and does not suggest that God in particular has witnessed the event and plans to intervene. But when an authorship — also in the Mishnah — speaks of a wife's being accused of unfaithfulness to her husband, by contrast, that authorship expects that God will intervene in this particular case in the required ordeal and so declare a decision for the case at hand. In the former instance, God is assuredly a premise of discourse, having revealed in the Torah the rule governing a goring ox. In the latter, God is not only premise but very present in discourse and in making a decision. God furthermore constitutes a person in certain settings, not in others.

3. One may readily envisage God as premise without invoking a notion of the particular traits or personality of God. So too, in the case of God as presence, no aspect of the case at hand demands that we specify particular attitudes or traits of character to be imputed to God. But there is a setting in which God is held always to know and pay attention to specific cases, and that involves God as a "you," that is, as a presence. For example, all discourse concerning liturgy in the Mishnah (obviously not only in that document) understands that God also hears prayer, and hence is not only a presence but a person, a

you, responding to what is said, requiring certain attitudes and rejecting others. In a later document, by contrast, God is not only present but a participant, if only implicitly, when the Torah is studied among disciples of sages. Here too we find an interesting indicator of how God is portrayed in one situation as a premise, in a second as a presence, and in a third as a person.

In cases in which God is portrayed as a person, however, there are rules and regulations to which God adheres. These permit us to imagine that God is present, without wondering what particular response God may make to a quite specific situation, e.g., within the liturgy. We do not have to wonder, because the rules tell us. Accordingly, while God is a liturgical "you," God as person still is not represented in full particularity, reaching a decision on a specific case in accord with traits of mind or heart or soul that express a unique personality, different (by nature) from all other personalities. God as person but not as personality remains within the framework established at the outset when we considered the matters of God as premise and as presence.

4. God emerges as a vivid and highly distinctive personality, actor, conversation-partner, hero. In references to God as a personality, God is given corporeal traits. God looks like God in particular, just as each person exhibits distinctive physical traits. Not only so, but in matters of heart and mind and spirit, well-limned individual traits of personality and action alike endow God with that particularity that identifies every individual human being. When God is given attitudes but no active role in discourse, referred to but not invoked as part of a statement, God serves as person. When God participates as a hero and protagonist in a narrative, God gains traits of personality and emerges as God like humanity: God incarnate.

The Hebrew Scriptures had long ago portrayed God in richly personal terms: God wants, cares, demands, regrets, says, and does — just like human beings. In the written Torah God is not merely a collection of abstract theological attributes and thus rules for governance of reality, nor a mere person to be revered and feared. God is not a mere composite of regularities, but a very specific, highly particular personality, whom people can know, envision, engage, persuade, impress. Sages painted this portrait of a personality by making up narratives, telling stories in which God figures like other (incarnate) heroes. When, therefore, the authorships of documents of the canon of the oral half of the dual Torah began to represent God as personality, not merely premise, presence, or person, they reentered that realm of discourse about God that Scripture had originally laid out. It was inevitable that some sages, represented by the authorship of the Bavli, should have done so.

True, that legacy of Scripture's God as actor and personality constituted for the sages — who in the first six centuries C.E. created the Judaism of the dual Torah — an available treasury of established facts about God, God incarnate. But within the books and verses of Scripture sages picked and chose, and they did so with regard to God as well. At some points in the unfolding corpus, without regard to the entire range of available facts of Scripture, God was represented only as implicit premise, in others, as presence and source of action, in still others as person. So the repertoire of Scripture tells us solely what might have been. It was only at the end, in the Bavli, that we reach what did come about, which is the portrayal, much as in Scripture and on the strength of Scripture's facts, of God as personality, with that same passionate love for Israel that, as Scripture's authorships had portrayed matters, had defined God in the received, written Torah.

In common discourse, when people speak about God, they assume they are supposed to prove the existence of God. But Judaism in its classical age never found it necessary to do so. The reason is that, since God is known through the Torah, sages recognize no need to prove the existence of God. The Torah proves the existence of God, and the glories of the natural world demonstrate the workings of God in the world. What humanity must do is explore what it means to be "in our image, after our likeness," that is, to be "like God." That is the more difficult but more important task: how to make ourselves worthy of being described "in our image, after our likeness." The sages bear the task of setting forth, through the oral Torah that they transmit, precisely the answer to that question: how should humanity form itself to be "in God's image," "after God's likeness," and what does that mean?

What we shall see, therefore, is that the Babylonian Talmud represents God in the flesh in the analogy of the human person. Prior to the Bavli, the faithful encountered God as abstract premise, as unseen presence, as a "you" without richly defined traits of soul, body, spirit, mind, or feeling. The Bavli's authorship for the first time in the formation of Judaism presented God as a fully formed personality, like a human being in corporeal traits, attitudes, emotions, and other virtues, in actions and the means of carrying out actions. God then looked the way human beings look, felt and responded the way they do, and performed the actions that they perform in the ways in which they perform them. And yet in that portrayal of the character of divinity, God always remained God. The insistent comparison of God with humanity "in our image and likeness" comes to its conclusion in one sentence that draws humanity upward and does not bring God downward. For, despite its treatment of the sage as a holy man, the Bavli's characterization of God never confused God with a sage or a sage with God. Quite to the contrary, the point and purpose of that characterization reaches its climax in a story that in powerful language demands that in the encounter with the sage of all sages God be left to be God.

Incarnation in Christianity: God Made Manifest in Jesus Christ

The Incarnation is both the most obvious and the most opaque feature of Christian faith. It is the most obvious, because the reference to Jesus as being God distinguishes Christianity radically from other religions. And it is the most opaque, because that reference, which is an axiom for believers, simply makes no sense to those outside the perspective of Christianity. The earliest depiction of the crucifixion is in fact a crude insult, scrawled on a wall in Rome. It shows a supplicant before a crucified ass, with the caption, "Alexamenos says: Worship God." That is eloquent reminder of the opacity of Christian faith to outsiders, even during the second century.[1]

---

1 For a photograph and a brief description, see Jean Daniélou and Henri Marrou, *The Christian Centuries*, vol. 1: *The First Six Hundred Years*, trans.

Our immediate purpose here is to show that the Incarnation is a fundamental reference within Christianity rather than a late speculative doctrine. The instructional source of Jesus' sayings which has been called "Q" takes on the programmatic issue of who Jesus is. One saying in particular has long attracted critical attention (Matt. 11:25b–27; Luke 10:21–22):

> I acknowledge to you, father, lord of heaven and earth, that you have hidden these things from the wise and intelligent, and revealed them to babes. Yes, father, for so it was pleasing before you. Everything is given me by my father, and no one knows the son except the father, neither does anyone know the father except the son, and anyone to whom the son wishes to reveal him.

The setting of the saying in the instructional source is a series of denunciations against those who have rejected the message of Jesus and his followers (Matt. 11:20–24; Luke 10:12–15, cf. vv. 16–20). In contrast to those whose arrogance blinds them to a simple truth, the saying contrasts the "babes" (*nepioi*).

The metaphor builds upon the axiom, well established within the Gospels, that in order to enter the kingdom one must receive it as a child receives: without inhibition, completely absorbed by the vision of what is sought (Matt. 19:13–15 and 18:3; Mark 10:13–16; Luke 18:15–17).[2] What is commended about children in such sayings is not their romantic innocence (a theme that ill accords with the skepticism of antiquity); rather, their naive, single-minded desire is commended as a good model for how to enter the kingdom. A due sense of proportion is precisely what prevents the wise and intelligent from the revelation which the naifs might enjoy.

The "babes" are defined in a specific fashion as those to whom the son chooses to reveal the father. The relationship between father and son is the generative point of the saying. Each is the sole and sufficient criterion of who the other is; within

---

V. Cronin, illustrations by P. Ludlow (New York: McGraw-Hill, 1964), plate 10. My construal of the Greek in fact differs from that presentation.

2. For a consideration, see McDonald's treatment in Bruce Chilton and J. I. H. McDonald, *Jesus and the Ethics of the Kingdom* (London: SPCK, 1987; Grand Rapids: Eerdmans, 1988), 83–89.

that circle of intimacy, "babes" are included by incorporation because the son reveals the truth to them. By the time we come to the end of the saying, "babes" is no longer even a metaphor of human temperament, but a way of speaking of how believers are related to God the father through Christ.

The whole of the teaching turns, then, around the circular relationship of mutual knowledge between father and son. In a manner even more radical that in the story concerning Peter's confession (see Matt. 16:13–20; Mark 8:27–30; Luke 9:18–21), any established title by which to measure Jesus (however exalted) is refused. Father and son are truly intelligible only to one another; anyone else is (at best) a fledgling adopted into the family circle. The pericope underscores its method by the lack of specification even as to whether the "son" is "of God" or "of man." The hearer is left to decide, and then to see that a decision between the alternatives is beside the point, because titles are deliberately transcended here. The instructional source insists upon the priority of a way of thinking about Jesus over any title that may be used of him. It proceeds from an insight concerning Jesus' relationship with God, which is the standard by which other understandings of Jesus are to be rejected or qualified.

The radicalism of the instructional source resides in its insistence upon the mutuality of the relationship. One might have predicted, on the basis of the story concerning Peter's confession, that Jesus might say that no one knows the son truly except the father. God can be the only valid standard of his own emissary. But the instructional source introduces what is not a corollary, but a statement of equivalent weight, that no one knows the father truly except the son. The Jesus of John's Gospel will say to his disciples (by way of a response to Thomas's question):

> I am the way and the truth and the life; no one comes to the father except through me. If you knew me, you will know my father, and from this moment you do know him and have seen him. (14:6–7)

The inescapable implication, that seeing Jesus is seeing the father, is spelled out in an exchange with Philip (vv. 8–9).

Johannine christology picks up and expands upon the symmetrical and mutual relationship of father and son, which is a feature of "Q."

The instructional saying manifests what is commonly regarded as a "high" christology, precisely in that the relationship is fully mutual and not a matter of the subordination of Jesus to the father. Commentators for better than a century have come to call the passage the "Johannine meteorite," as if it were unexpected so early within the traditions behind the Gospels. The terminology betrays the christology of the liberal critics themselves. They suppose that Jesus must originally have thought of himself simply as anointed by God — in the sense of being dispatched for a purpose — and that pious imagination provided the rest.

C. F. D. Moule has summarized the liberal consensus, and goes on to remark:

> And it does, at first sight, look like an easy bridge for the fancy to traverse: starting from a human, messianic Son, it crosses over to a divine, transcendental Son.[3]

There are, however, two gaping holes in the bridge. The first is that the tradition rings hollow just when it concerns using "messiah" as an adequate category for Jesus, as the story of Peter's confession shows. It could be used as a title only after it had been defined anew; Moule observes that "Jesus could scarcely have been styled Messiah (or Christ) after his crucifixion at all unless his friends had already become convinced that he was Messiah in some unusual and transcendental sense."

Because Moule is both a skilled exegete and a theologian of Anglican doctrine, his terms of reference in the article (and elsewhere) are doctrinal. Specifically, he wishes to know whether the earliest of christologies was "evolutionary," crossing the "easy bridge" he describes, or "transcendental," that is, animated by the conviction that Jesus is " 'one in being' with God." His contribution to the study of christology is one of

---

3. "Incarnation: Paradox That Will Not Go Away," *The Times Higher Education Supplement* (December 23, 1977): 11.

the most important in this century, because he has revealed the reflexive recourse to an evolutionary point of view among interpreters, and he has suggested an exegetically viable alternative. Perhaps the greatest tribute to his contribution is that it has been consistently sidestepped in a doctrinal discussion which has proceeded along the party lines of liberals and conservatives.

Here, then, is an example of the arid debate between liberals and conservatives to which we have called attention within this trilogy. Liberals are so committed to an evolutionary approach, they ignore its exegetical problems. Conservatives are so afraid that critical inquiry will let them down, they prefer simply to assert inerrancy and leave the connection between Scripture and belief unexplored. In their respective campaigns of programmatic silence, an interpreter of the first order has been largely ignored just as he was making a most seminal contribution.

From the perspective of a generative exegesis in search of an understanding of Christianity as a system of religion, Moule's critique of the liberal consensus is of the first importance. His own alternative, however, which he styles the "transcendental" christology of Christian orthodoxy, must not be immediately invoked. The antinomy between the two is, to begin with, typical of the tension between science and orthodoxy which has entranced and obsessed intellectual observers since the nineteenth century. The antinomy may prove to be important within the New Testament, and therefore of merit in understanding the development of christology, or it may turn out to be an artifact of a division between faith and reason which is characteristic of intellectuals only since the Enlightenment.

We would therefore reformulate Moule's criticism of the liberal consensus. Instead of invoking an allegedly transcendental assessment of Jesus among the disciples, we have seen simply that the Petrine confession insists that no single term, not even "Christ," may be accurately used of Jesus, unless it is redefined in the light of knowledge of Jesus himself. Jesus is the term of reference which determines the propriety of a title, not the reverse, because Jesus' relationship to God is what makes and unmakes the relevance of the title. For Jesus' relationship, the instructional source goes on to insist, is more *with* God than to God: father and son constitute a circle of intimacy in comparison with which all else is subsidiary, and into which one may be included only by the grace of revelation. The first hole in the evolutionary bridge is that the term "messiah," the postulated point of departure, offers no easy transition to such a notion. Indeed, we might go a bit further than Moule and suggest that it is possible to appreciate the Petrine confession and Jesus' acknowledgment of his father only when terms such as "messiah" are qualified to the point of redefinition.

That brings us to the second hole in the evolutionary bridge, which is — if anything — even more gaping than the first. There are simply too many titles applied to Jesus within too short a space of time to sustain the argument that one title spawned the rest. Moreover, there is no reason to suppose such titles would have had to have been manufactured simply because Jesus was effective as a teacher or reputed for unusual deeds. Several brilliant rabbis taught during the first century, some of them skilled in healing and a few of them credited with an ability to influence natural phenomena; they managed to do so without being called "messiah," "son of God," "son of man," or the like. A few revolutionary figures are styled "false prophets" by Josephus, and the famous messianic pretender of the second century, Simeon bar Kosiba, styled himself Bar Kokhba ("son of the star," after Num. 24:17) in order to proclaim his invincible might. But the untitled precedents far outweighed the titled, and insofar as titles are invoked, they signal a political and military power which Jesus never commanded.

A doctrinal approach such as Moule's infers from such evidence that Jesus himself must have been very different from his contemporaries, that there was a "transcendental" dimension within his person which escaped categorization, and yet which resonated — however partially — with the primary categories of how God was expected definitively to act through a single person on behalf of humanity. A systemic approach must eschew reference to the transcendent, except as such reference might emerge in the system to hand. The systemic impact of Peter's confession and Jesus' acclamation of his father's revelation is to make the relationship between Jesus and God the point from which any assessment of Jesus is to be generated, and at the same time the only means of access to God.

Within the discussion which follows, we will analyze distinct visions of God in the world. In the analysis of Christianity, the result will be that the precedents of the Incarnation and its development within the terms of reference of prayer will be uncovered. By the close of the period of the New Testament, the language of ontology was used in order to explain the Incarnation, a language best instanced in Colossians.

The Paul of Colossians speaks through the mouth of Timothy (see 1:1), probably around the year 90 C.E. Timothy's Paul directly asserts Jesus' existence prior to any historical appearance (1:15–20):

He is the invisible God's image, firstborn of all creation, because everything was created by him, in heaven and on earth, visible and invisible.

Be they angelic thrones or lordships or principalities or authorities, everything has been created through him and for him.

He is before all things, and all things consist in him, and he is the head of the body, the Church.

He is the beginning, firstborn of the dead, that he might personally be precedent in all things. For in him all the fullness was pleased to dwell, and through him — and for him — to reconcile all things (whether on earth or in heaven), as he made peace through the blood of his cross.

The advanced nature of the passage is manifest, not only in its development of language also used in John's Gospel, but in its development of typically Pauline expressions. The Church as the body of Christ, a concept that had been used by Paul himself to insist that all Christians belong to one another in Christ,[4] here is applied in the sense of a hierarchy, to insist that Christ is the head. And the Pauline emphasis upon the importance of reconciliation between people as a function of their salvation

---

4. See 1 Corinthians 12:12–27; Romans 12:4–8.

in Christ[5] here reaches into the truly cosmic dimensions of the powers behind the visible world.

Colossians reaches into the treasury of early Christian theology in order to fashion a true christology: an ontology of Jesus Christ as God. The very person who died on the cross is the origin and the goal of the entire creation; he is the primordial first instance, the inherent principle of order, and the proleptic end point of all things. Orthodox Christianity in the centuries after the formation of the New Testament would avail itself of the language and thought of Colossians in order to agree upon creedal confessions of christology. The length, complication, and violence of the struggle for creedal unity amount to an old story, which cannot be rehearsed here.

Uncompromising and trenchant though Colossians is in its claim of Jesus' divinity, at one point there is a certain obscurity. Which "fullness" is it which chooses to dwell in him (1:19)? It would *seem* to be the divine fullness, which also is to reconcile all things in Christ, but there may be a certain ambiguity. If so, Colossians later removes it, in a passage which begins by discussing the ethical implications of baptism (2:6–11a):

> As you, then, received Christ Jesus the Lord, walk in him, rooted and built up in him and established in faith — just as you were taught, abounding in thanksgiving. See to it lest anyone make prey of you by means of philosophy and empty deceit: the tradition of men and the elements of the world, and not Christ. For in him all the fullness of deity dwells bodily, and you are fulfilled in him, who is the head of every principality and authority. In him also you were circumcised with a circumcision made without hands. . . .

If there were some ambiguity in the earlier statement about the "fullness," now it is exploited, because it is asserted both that believers are fulfilled in Christ Jesus and — more dramatically — that deity resides bodily in him.

For all that the claim is plain, it is also not without complexity. The language of "body" has already been deployed to

---

5. See 2 Corinthians 5:14–21; Romans 5:10. The term Paul preferred was *katalasso;* in Ephesians (2:16) and Colossians (1:20, 22) it becomes *apokatalasso.*

speak of the Church of which Christ is head (see also 1:24; 2:10, and vv. 16–19) so that believers' endowment with "Christ in you" (1:27) is also an indwelling of God in their midst. But the "bodily" indwelling of God is not merely a metaphorical way to speak of the Church. "Body" is also meant literally, as when Colossians states that Christ has "reconciled [you] by the body of his flesh through death" (1:22). Deity is first of all resident there "bodily," and on that basis may be said to dwell in the Church as well.

The fundamental response to the issue of christology, then, is ontological. Jesus Christ speaks of God, teaches God's way, conveys divine grace, transforms human life, offers access to the kingdom, simply because he is God. There is a functionally infinite variety of ways to speak of Christ's being as God, and the reverse, and serious differences are bound to emerge as that variety is realized. But that the range of ways God is reflected in Christ can be explained fully only by relating Christ and deity essentially — and not simply by representing Christ as correct in certain of his opinions about God — is an assertion which is characteristic of Christianity.

The relational sonship of "Q" and the ontological Incarnation of Colossians would seem logically to be akin to one another. To understand that kinship, to see the progression of the Incarnation from Jesus' teaching to a fundamental doctrine of Christianity, is the purpose of our discussion in chapters 4 through 6. As we make our way in that understanding, we will be mapping the history of the movement which would become Christianity, and also assessing its systemic center.

Part One

Knowing God
in the Torah

JACOB NEUSNER

The Mishnah's God
of the Philosophers

People who think that we may know God entirely on our own, discovering God for the first time when we get up in the morning, treat the knowledge of God as personal and private. But in Judaism we do not discover God on our own, nor is the knowledge of God accessible only or mainly through our individual experience. Because we have the Torah as the record of what God says to us, we always know God not by ourselves alone. We know God through the Torah, that is, by means of the access of the holy people Israel to the record of God's revelation in the Torah. The Torah comes to us all, in community. There — in community — we learn what God is and does and wants of us. Our knowledge of God is traditional, in that it is handed down from generation to generation, as much as it is immediate; it is public and communal as much as it is personal and individual; we know God, we and not only I.

We pray to God always as "we," even when we are by ourselves, because our quest for God is not private, new and without precedent, or subjective. It always is a quest as Israel, the holy people, to whom God as an act of surpassing love and grace gave the Torah. So our meeting with God is public. It comes from generation to generation, always surprising, yet always reliable. And it is objective: God calls, we respond, and the act of faith attests to the invitation to faith. Ours is not a leap of faith. Ours is a response to a God who, because God calls, provokes us to wonder. That is why, in the theology of Judaism, the right question about God is not whether or not

God exists, nor even what God is like, but rather what God wants of me and how within holy Israel, the Jewish people, I can make myself into what the Torah says I am, which is in God's image and after God's likeness. That is why our quest for God begins — though it does not end — in the Torah, written and oral alike. Any account of what the theology of Judaism teaches about God, therefore, must begin in that same place, and that accounts for the character of this anthology.

Then who is God, the God who calls and to whom we respond? In Judaism God comes to us in terms we human beings can grasp, even though what we say about God — creator of heaven and earth — refers to God beyond time, beyond space, beyond all conceiving. God in Judaism is incarnate by reason of the gift of the Torah. That is to tell us that God is described "in the image, after the likeness" of humanity. The conception of humanity in the image of God then portrays God as a human being, a sublime idea that will not for one minute have surprised the authors of a variety of Judaic documents, beginning with the compilers of the Pentateuch. Some speaking explicitly, others in subtle allusions, prophets and apocalyptic writers, exegetes and sages, mystics and legists, all maintained that notion. No single genre of writing — law, prophecy, wisdom, history — ever exercised a monopoly over the presentation of God described for us in the categories we grasp in this world: we are like God, and so we can understand God like us. Now to the first stage in the re-presentation of God: the God of the philosophers.

The writing down of the originally oral part of the Torah begins with the Mishnah, a philosophical law book brought to closure at ca. 200 C.E. and later on called the first statement of the oral Torah. In its wake, the Mishnah drew tractate Abot, ca. 250 C.E., a statement concluded a generation after the Mishnah on the standing of the authorities of the Mishnah; Tosefta, ca. 300 C.E., a compilation of supplements of various kinds to the statements in the Mishnah; and two systematic exegeses of books of Scripture or the written Torah, Sifra, on Leviticus, Sifré on Numbers, and another Sifré, on Deuteronomy, of indeterminate date but possibly concluded by 300 C.E.

In the Mishnah — as in all other writings of Judaism — God

is present not merely in details, when actually mentioned, but at the foundations. To characterize the encounter with God, whether intellectual or concrete and everyday, we must therefore pay attention not alone to passages that speak of God in some explicit way, but, even more so, to the fundamental givens on which all particular doctrines or stories of a document depend. What that fact means in the case of the Mishnah is simple. That great philosophical law code demonstrates over and over again that all things are one, that complex things yield uniform and similar components, and that, rightly understood, there is a hierarchy of being, to be discovered through the proper classification of all things. What this means is that, for the philosophers who wrote the Mishnah, the most important thing they wished to demonstrate about God is that God is one. And this they proposed to prove by showing, in a vast array of everyday circumstances, (1) the fundamental order and unity of all things, all being, and (2) the unity of all things in an ascending order to God. So all things through their unity and order are directed to one thing, and all being derives from One God.

In the Mishnah, many things are placed into sequence and order — "hierarchized" — and the order of all things is shown to have a purpose, so that the order, or hierarchization, is purposive, or "teleological." The Mishnah time and again demonstrates these two contrary propositions: (1) many things join together by their nature into one thing, and (2) one thing yields many things. These propositions of course complement each other, because, in forming matched opposites, the two set forth an ontological judgment. It is that all things are not only orderly, but, in their deepest traits of being, so are ordered that many things fall into one classification, and one thing may hold together many things of a single classification. For this philosophy, then, rationality consists in the hierarchy of the order of things, a rationality tested and proved, time and again, by the possibility always of effecting the hierarchical classification of all things. The Mishnah's proposition, then, is a theory of the right ordering of each thing in its classification (or taxon), with all the categories (or taxa) in correct sequence, from least to greatest. And showing that all things can be ordered and that all orders can be set into relationship with one another, we transform the ontological message into its components of proposition, argument, and demonstration.

The sustained effort of the authorship of the Mishnah, therefore, is to demonstrate how many classes of things — actions, relationships, circumstances, persons, places — really form one class. This work of classification, then, explores the potentialities of chaos — but that exploration is a journey en route to explicit order. It is classification transformed from the *how* of intellection to the *why* and the *what for* and, above all, the *what does it all mean* of philosophical conviction. And the goal is to show, through the very qualities of the natural and social world, that all things point to the plan and purpose of the one God, who so ordered creation as to reveal the divine plan for a well-ordered world: everything in its proper place, each with its rightful name, all things in the order in which, in six days, they were made.

Recognition that one thing may fall into several categories and many things into a single one comes to expression, for the authorship of the Mishnah, in a simple way. The authorship shows over and over again that diversity in species or diversification in actions follows orderly lines, thus confirming the claim that there is that single point from which many lines come forth. Carried out in proper order (1) the many form one thing and (2) one thing yields many; the demonstration then leaves no doubt as to the truth of the matter.

The upshot may be stated very simply. The species point to the genus, the classes to one class, all classes of things, or taxa, properly hierarchized then rise to the top of the structure and the system forming one taxon. So all things ascend to and reach one thing. All that remains is for the philosopher to define that one thing: God. But that is a step that the philosophers of the Mishnah did not take, at least not in an articulated way. I assume that the reason is that they did not think they had to make such an obvious point. But I think there is a further and altogether different reason. It is because, as a matter of fact, they were philosophers who were not theologians at all. The document they produced pursues issues of natural history, never working out a proposition of a theological character — not in a single line! And to philosophers, while God serves as premise and principle, the system does not derive its generative problematic from that fact. It is not that on which the system-builders propose to work.

By showing that all things can be ordered and that all orders can be set into relationship with one another, we transform method into message. The message of hierarchical classification is that many things really form a single thing, the many species a single genus, the many genera an encompassing and well-crafted, cogent whole. Every time we speciate, we affirm that position; each successful labor of forming relationships among species, e.g., making them into a genus, or identifying the hierarchy of the species, proves it again. Not only so, but when we can show that many things are really one or that one thing yields many (the reverse and confirmation of the former), we express in a fresh way a single immutable truth, the truth of this philosophy concerning the unity of all being in an orderly composition of all things within a single taxon.

To philosophers, as I said at the outset, God serves as premise and principle (and whether or not it is one God or many gods, a unique being or a being that finds a place in a class of similar beings hardly is germane!), and philosophy serves not to demonstrate principles or to explore premises, but to analyze the unknown, to answer important questions.

In such an enterprise the premise, God, turns out to be merely instrumental, and the given principle, to be merely interesting. But for philosophers, intellectuals, God can live not in the details, but in the unknowns, in the as yet unsolved problem and the unresolved dilemma. So, I think, in the Mishnah, God lives, so to speak, in the excluded middle, is revealed in the interstitial case, is made known through the phenomena that form a single phenomenon, is perceived in the one that is many, is encountered in the many that are one. For that is the dimension of being — that, so I claim, immanental and sacramental dimension of being — that defines for this philosophy its statement of ultimate concern, its recurrent point of tension, its generative problematic. That then is the urgent question, the ineluctable and self-evidently truthful answer: God in the form, God in the order, God in the structure, God in the heights, God at the head of the great chain of well-ordered being, in its proper hierarchy. True, God is premise, scarcely mentioned. But it is because God's name does not have to be mentioned when the whole of the order of being says that name, and only that name, and always that name, the Name unspoken because it is always in the echo, the silent, thin voice, the numinous in all phenomena of relationship: the interstitial God of the Mishnah.

Like eighteenth-century Deists, the Mishnah's philosophers focus upon the government by the rule and law that God has set forth in the Torah. Taking slight, and then merely episodic, interest in God's particular and ad hoc intervention into the smooth application of the now-paramount regularities of the law, that authorship rarely represented God as an immediate — therefore ad hoc and episodic and by definition irregular — presence, let alone person. That sort of intervention by God is invoked only in one instance known to me, as I shall suggest in a moment. The Mishnah's authorship rarely decided a rule or a case by appealing to God's presence and choice particular to that rule or case.

That is to say, God not as premise but immediate presence does not very often play an everyday and active role in the Mishnah's processes and system of decision-making. To take two stunning examples, in the entire division of Purities, which encompasses more than a quarter of the Mishnah in volume, I cannot point to a single passage in which God's presence forms a consideration of cleanness or uncleanness, susceptibility or insusceptibility to uncleanness, in the statement or application of a rule. The rules of susceptibility to and contracting of uncleanness, as well as those of removing that uncleanness, work themselves out without appeal to God's will or person. That is the case, even though the division attends to laws meant by the priestly authorship of Leviticus and Numbers to protect the cult from the danger of uncleanness. A survey of the civil code presented in the tractates Baba Qama, Baba Mesia, and Baba Batra, covering the transactions of commerce, real estate, torts, damages, labor law, and the like, in the aggregate, correspond to civil law in our own society, yields not a single appeal to God's presence or God's ad hoc intervention into a case. All things are governed by regularities and norms, such that God has no place in the everyday world of mortals' exchanges and interchanges.

While God forms the prevailing premise of discourse, that fact makes slight difference in what is said. The Mishnah's God is a God of philosophers.

The full weight of the character of the Mishnah's portrayal of the character of divinity will make its mark only when we have taken the measure of the Talmuds' God — both the Yerushalmi's and the Bavli's. There the contrast between God as essentially a premise of all being and God as an active personality engaged in everyday transactions with specific persons will lend immediacy to these now-general observations. But even in the Mishnah an exception to the rule of God as formal premise of being highlights the rule.

The generative force of the Mishnah's system — the active power that makes the system work, frames its questions, and dictates its answers — is the human attitude and intention. That is the point at which, ordinarily, the Mishnah also invokes God's presence. That is to say, God's presence forms the presupposition of those rules that attend to human attitude during the performance of certain religious actions, e.g., the recitation of obligatory prayers. The obligation to recite the *Shema* encompasses the requirement "to direct one's heart," which is to say, to recite the required words with the intention of fulfilling one's duty to recite those words (M. Ber. 2:1). One's attitude is taken into account in diverse other ways, e.g., not reciting the *Shema* under circumstances that will prevent one from forming the right attitude, such as when one has to bury a deceased relative (M. Ber. 3:1). So too, when reciting the Prayer (the Eighteen Benedictions), it must be in a sober attitude (M. Ber. 5:1), and particular piety requires an hour of inner preparation, "that they may direct their heart toward God" (M. Ber. 5:1).

> One may stand to pray only in a solemn frame of mind.
>
> The early pious ones used to tarry one hour [before they would] pray, so that they could direct their hearts to the Omnipresent.
>
> [While one is praying] even if the king greets him, he may not respond.
>
> And even if a serpent is entwined around his heel, he may not interrupt [his prayer].

They refer to the "wonder of the rain" in [the blessing concerning] "the resurrections of the dead" [the second blessing in the Eighteen Benedictions].

And they ask for the rains in "the blessings of the years" [the ninth blessing].

And [they insert] habdalah in [the blessing which concludes] "endower of knowledge" [the fourth blessing].

R. Aqiba says, "One says it as a fourth blessing unto itself."

R. Eliezer says, "[One says it] in the 'thanksgiving' [the Eighteenth Blessing]."

[As for] one who says, "May thy mercy reach the nest of a bird" or "For good may your name be mentioned," "We give thanks, we give thanks" — they silence him.

[As for] one who comes before the ark [to recite the liturgy on behalf of the congregation] and erred — let another go before [the ark] in his place.

And [the one designated as a replacement] may not decline at this time.

Whence does [the replacement] begin?

At the beginning of the blessing in which the [previous] one erred.

One who goes before the ark [to lead the prayer] shall not answer "Amen" after the [blessing of the] priests.

Because [he might become] confused [and not know where to begin again].

And [even] if there is no priest present besides himself [the leader], he should not raise his hands [as normally is done by priests who recite the priestly blessing].

But if he is sure that he can raise his hands [to recite the priestly blessing] and return to his prayer, he is permitted [to do so].

He who prays and errs — it is a bad sign for him.

And if he is communal agent [who prays on behalf of the whole congregation], it is a bad sign for them that appointed him.

[This is on the principle that] a man's agent is like [the man] himself.

They said concerning R. Haninah b. Dosa, "When he would pray for the sick he would say, 'This one shall live' or 'This one shall die.' "

They said to him, "How do you know?"

He said to them, "If my prayer is fluent, then I know that it is accepted [and the person will live].

"But if not, I know that it is rejected [and the person will die]."

M. Berakhot 5:1–4

It must follow that there is a presence to assess the recitation of the correct words with the correct attitude. That presence is not material; one fulfills the obligation even though the words are not said sufficiently loud to be heard, even by the one who says them (M. Ber. 2:3). But it is physical, in the sense that God is assumed to be located in one place rather than in some other. Accordingly, one recites prayers facing a particular location, namely, Jerusalem, and if one cannot do so in a physical way, at least one does so in the heart, directing the heart "toward the Holy of Holies" (M. Ber. 4:6). That God is conceived to be located in the Holy of Holies is underlined by the rule that one should not conduct oneself in an inappropriate way while opposite the Temple's eastern gate, which faces the Holy of Holies (M. Ber. 9:5). It goes without saying that God hears and answers statements made in any language, not only in Hebrew, although Hebrew is the holy and preferred language for certain formulas (M. Sot. 7:1).

God's presence is signified by the character of the occasion as well, e.g., the number and splendor of those present. Rules covering the recitation of prayers took account of the size of the group and importance of those present on the occasion. If three are present for the Grace after Meals, one begins, "Bless the one of whose bounty we have partaken," if there are ten, "Bless our God...," and onward up to ten thousand: "We will bless the Lord our God, the God of Israel, the God of hosts, who sits between the Cherubim, for the food we have eaten..." (M. Ber. 7:3). But this is a minor point. The main consideration is that God responds to the human will and expression of human intentionality. That becomes especially clear when we see how God hears statements of what a human being wishes, or does not wish, joined to an act of consecration or sanctification through human words: vows, oaths, statements of sanctification and dedication, and the like. Here is where the encounter between God and the human person takes place: in the human being's action and volition.

God hears not only prayers offered by the community but also vows and oaths taken by individuals. That is the foundation of the tractates on vows (Nedarim), oaths (Shabuot), oaths of valuation of another person such as are specified in Leviticus 27:1ff. (Arakhin), and the special vow of the Nazirite (Num. 6:1–21, tractate Nazir). To this list we may add numerous tractates that presuppose that God (directly or through angels or other messengers) confirms the stated intention of a human being. These include, for example, Temurah's rules on designating gifts to the altar or to the upkeep of the Temple house and Terumot's rules (representative of an equivalent premise governing tractates Peah, Demai, Maaserot, Maaser Sheni, Hallah, and Bikkurim) on the designation of a portion of the crop for God's share and use, and the like. The mere utterance of the appropriate words invokes, for the person who says them, a vow or an oath (depending on the formula, purpose, and occasion); such a statement then is binding and imposes concrete obligations of acts of commission or omission. A vow commonly declares a secular object to be holy, e.g., imposing upon food the status of God's food upon the altar, and, in consequence, one who has imputed to the food a sacred status may not consume such food. God then is assumed not only to have heard, but also to have taken account of the vow or oath, which again implies immediacy and presence under all circumstances. God furthermore will take into account the attitude of mind or intentionality associated with a verbal expression, so that there are vows that are not binding, e.g., those of incitement, exaggeration, error, and constraint (M. Ned. 3:1). In such cases the statement is null; God knows the difference. The same principles in general apply to the special vow of the Nazirite.

It goes without saying that God knows not only public deeds, but also secret ones, as much as intentions. Consequently, God will settle the matter of a husband's jealousy of his wife by guiding the working of the bitter water in such a way as to show what, if anything, has actually taken place (Num. 5:11–31, tractate Sotah). God's involvement in the rite is direct, since the name of God is written on the scroll prepared for the rite and then blotted out in the water that the woman has to drink. The oath that is imposed, of course, contains the expected implication that God hears oaths and punishes those who take an oath in vain. In all of these aspects, God forms a powerful presence, if a systemically inert one, guaranteeing rules but not exhibiting distinctive traits. But the philosopher's conception of God competes in the Mishnah with yet another.

The authorship of the Tosefta, a supplement to the Mishnah, which flourished about a century after the completion of the Mishnah in ca. 200, presents materials of three kinds: direct citation and gloss of the Mishnah's sentences; exegesis, without direct citation, of the Mishnah's sentences in discussions that are fully comprehensible only by reference to the Mishnah; and statements that deal with the subject matter of the Mishnah but are fully comprehensible without reference to the Mishnah. The first two types predominate.

The Tosefta appeals for order, structure, and program to the Mishnah's tractate. The presence of God, referred to by the word *Shekhinah,* makes an explicit appearance in T. Men. 7:8B–F, with reference to the verse, "Moses saw all the work ... and Moses blessed them" (Exod. 39:43): "With what blessing did he bless them? He said to them, 'May the presence of God dwell with the work of your hands. ... ' " And further,"Just as you have been engaged in the work of making the tabernacle and the presence of God has dwelled with the work of your hands, so may you have the merit of building before me the chosen house, and may the presence of God dwell with the work of your hands." God's presence is furthermore acknowledged by the "you" of the liturgy, e.g., "May your will be done in heaven above, and grant ease to those that fear you" (T. Ber. 3:7C, among numerous instances), so too, "May it be your will ... " (T. Ber. 6:2C, among many instances). God's presence (*Shekhinah*) is further said to depart from Israel because of the sin of murder (T. Yoma 1:12, Sheb. 1:4) or because of tale-bearing (T. Sot. 14:3). The Presence waited upon various persons (T. Sot. 4:7).

The confession for the Day of Atonement (T. Yoma 2:1, 4:14) forms another occasion for acknowledging God's presence. Rules for reciting benedictions, e.g., in the Prayer, are spelled out also in the Tosefta (T. Ber. 1:4ff.), with some to be marked by genuflection, others not. These rules again rest on the conviction that God is present when prayers are said. But the presence of God was not the sole consideration; the convenience of the community at large made a difference. By himself, Aqiba would pray slowly and at length; with the community he did not take so long (T. Ber. 3:5).

God as a person whom one might envisage and even see formed the subject of interpretation of Ezekiel's vision of the Chariot (Ezek. 1:4), but the framers of the Mishnah merely allude to that fact (M. Hag. 2:1) and do not tell us the substance of the vision of God as a physical person. God's person, not merely God's presence, however, forms the presupposition of all acts of the recitation of prayer, which take for granted that God not only hears prayer but also cares about what the human being requests. One example, among many, is the prayer of the high priest on the Day of Atonement: "O God, your people, the house of Israel, have committed iniquity, transgressed and sinned before you. O God, forgive the iniquities and transgressions and sins which your people, the house of Israel, have committed . . . as it is written in the Torah of your servant, Moses, 'For on this day shall atonement be made for you to clean you, from all your sins shall you be clean before the Lord (Lev. 16:30)' " (M. Yoma. 6:2). God is everywhere a "you," and therefore a person.

Moreover, but, as a person God is assumed to respond to words and events much as human beings do. For example, when the community suffers from drought and prays for rain, God is not only asked to act as God had acted in times past, "May the one who answered our ancestors at the Red Sea answer you" (M. Ta. 2:4), but the acts of self-mortification and deprivation are meant to impress God and to win sympathy, much as they would (it was assumed) from a mortal ruler.

The manner of fasting: how [was it done]?
They bring forth the ark into the street of the town

and put wood ashes on (1) the ark, (2) the head of the patriarch, and (3) the head of the court.

And each person puts ashes on his head.

The eldest among them makes a speech of admonition: "Our brothers, concerning the people of Nineveh it is not said, 'And God saw their sackcloth and their fasting,' but, 'And God saw their deeds, for they repented from their evil way' " (Jonah 3:10).

And in prophetic tradition it is said, "Rend your heart and not your garments" (Joel 2:13).

They arise for prayer.

They bring down before the ark an experienced elder, who has children, and whose cupboard [house] is empty, so that his heart should be wholly in the prayer.

And he says before them twenty-four blessings: the eighteen said every day, and he adds six more to them.

And these are they: (1) Remembrance verses, (2) Shofar verses, (3) In my distress I cried to the Lord and he answered me (Ps. 120), (4) and, I will lift up my eyes to the hills... (Ps. 121), (5) Out of the depths I have cried to you, O Lord (Ps. 130), (6) and a prayer of the afflicted when he is overwhelmed (Ps. 102).

R. Judah says, "He did not have to say Remembrance verses and Shofar verses. But in their stead he says, (1) If there be in the land famine, if there be pestilence (1 Kings 8:37ff.). And (2) The word of the Lord which came to Jeremiah concerning the drought (Jer 14:1ff.). And he concludes each of them with its appropriate ending."

For the first [ending] he says, "He who answered Abraham on Mount Moriah will answer you and hear the sound of your cry this day. Blessed are you, O Lord, redeemer of Israel."

For the second he says, "He who answered our fathers at the Red Sea will answer you and hear the sound of your cry this day. Blessed are you, O Lord, who remembers forgotten things."

For the third he says, "He who answered Joshua at Gilgal will answer you and hear the sound of your cry this day. Blessed are you, O Lord, who hears the sound of the shofar."

For the fourth he says, "He who answered Samuel at Mispeh will answer you and hear the sound of your cry this day. Blessed are you, O Lord, who hears a cry."

For the fifth he says, "He who answered Elijah at Mount Carmel will answer you and hear the sound of your cry this day. Blessed are you, O Lord, who hears prayer."

For the sixth he says, "He who answered Jonah in the belly of the fish will answer you and hear the sound of your cry this day. Blessed are you, O Lord, who answers prayer in a time of trouble."

For the seventh he says, "He who answered David and Solomon, his son, in Jerusalem, will answer you and hear the sound of your cry this day. Blessed are you, O Lord, who has mercy on the Land."

M. Ta'anit 2:1–4

The one who represents the community in prayer was to be an elder who had children for whom to worry and a house empty of food (M. Ta. 2:2); such a one would be whole-hearted in the prayer. God would discern the sincerity and respond with sympathy. Hence God was understood as a person in whose model the human being had been made, and human beings, searching their own hearts, could understand God's.

Throughout the Mishnah we find that God hears and answers prayer, for example, "When I enter [the house of study], I pray that no offense will take place on my account, and when I leave, I give thanks for my lot" (M. Ber. 4:2). But that is not the end of the matter. Of still greater interest, God is assumed to take the form of a person, in the model of a heavenly monarch or emperor. For example, when one is reciting the Prayer, one is assumed to stand before the King and that location, in God's presence, requires appropriate probity: "Even if the king greets a person, one is not to reply, and even if a snake wrapped itself around one's heel, one is not to interrupt" (M. Ber. 5:1). The response to the recitation of prayer is not concrete personal engagement by God; there is no story in the Mishnah that suggests anyone believed God talked back to the one who said the prayer But there are explicit statements that God heard and answered prayer and so indicated on the spot, as we recall:

> They said of R. Haninah that, when he would say a prayer over the sick, he would say, "This one will live," or, "That one will die."
> They said to him, "How do you know?"
> He said to them, "If my prayer flows easily in my mouth, I know that it is accepted, and if not, I know that it is rejected."
>
> M. Ber. 5:5

God as "you" occurs not only in liturgy, but also in legal formulas recited upon specified occasions. Here, to be sure, the language, as much as the context, is defined by Scripture:

> "...I have removed...according to all your commandment which you have commanded me..." [Deut. 26: 13ff.]....
> "Look down from your holy habitation from heaven": We have done what you have decreed concerning us, now you do what you have promised to us...
>
> M. M.S. 5:10–13

The transaction is between two persons, each bound by the same rule that governs the other.

But the personhood of God as a "you" plays a role principally in the address of prayer. Scripture's portrait of God as an active personality finds no counterpart whatsoever in the Mishnah. The majestic presence of God in the unfolding of events, which forms the great theme of the scriptural narratives of ancient Israel's history, may define a premise of the Mishnah's worldview. But in no passage in the Mishnah does an action of God serve to explain an event, nor do we find lessons, as to God's purpose or will, drawn from events. Events take place, truths endure, but the two form a merely assumed and implicit relationship. In passages in which important events are catalogued, for example, God's action is not at issue. Interestingly, these events are always catalogued as completed actions in the past tense. They are described as changes of circumstance or situation, not decisions and actions of a divine monarch deciding from day to day what is to be done and then doing it:

> When the first prophets died, Urim and Thummim ceased. When the Temple was destroyed, the Shamir-worm ceased...and faithful men came to an end, as it is written, "Help, Lord, for the godly man ceases" (Ps. 12:1)....During the war of Vespasian, they forbade the crowns of the bridegrooms and the wedding drum. During the war of Titus, they forbade the crowns of the brides and that a man should teach his son Greek. In the last war they forbade the bride to go forth in a litter inside the city....When R. Meir died, there were no more makers of parables....
>
>   M. Sot. 9:12–15

Along these same lines, when in M. Zeb. 14:4–8, diverse periods in the history of the cult are specified, we find no invocation of the action or purpose of God. That is not to suggest that anyone imagined God had not done these things by decree. It is only to point out that the sorts of explicit conclusions drawn from historical events by the prophetic historians in Joshua, Judges, Samuel, and Kings, for example, find no counterpart in the Mishnah. God now *presides* as much as in the biblical narratives God truly ruled.

In the Tosefta's amplification of the Mishnah, God's communication with biblical figures is of course noted. God spoke with Moses, Abraham, Jacob, Samuel, and others (T. Ber. 12ff.), but these passages take for granted merely the facts of the biblical narrative. God's attitudes compare to those of mortals: "One in whom people take delight, God takes delight" (T. Ber. 3:3C). God is a person with emotions such as anger and mercy. So if when God is angry at the righteous, he has mercy on them, when he is disposed to be merciful, how much more does he have mercy on them! (T. Ber. 4:16J). God respects learning, of course, and is affronted when religious duties are carried out in an ignorant way (T. Ber. 6:18). The following saying of Hillel can be read as a statement imputed to God: "If you will come to my house, I shall come to your house. If you will not come to my house, I shall not come to your house, as it is said, 'In every place where I cause my name to be remembered I will come to you and bless you' (Exod. 20:24)" (T. Suk. 4:3B–D). If so, God is saying that those who come to the Temple will receive God in their houses, a clear indication of God as person, not merely premise or even presence.

God does not approve arrogance and favors the humble, a point repeatedly made in a review of the ancient history of creation: "The generation of the Flood acted arrogantly before the Omnipresent only on account of the good which he lavished on them.... The Omnipresent said to them, 'By the goodness which I lavished on them do they take pride before me? By that same good I shall exact punishment from them'" (Tos. Sot. 3:6–8; and so for the men of the Tower, Sodom, Egyptians, Samson, Absalom, Sennacherib, Nebuchadnezzar, T. Sot. 3:9–19). The statement attributed to God is not representative of a conversation with a vivid personality; rather it is an observation of a merely theological character, that is, the rendering in conversation form of the principle that God exacts punishment for arrogance and ingratitude, and does so through that very matter that brings up the arrogance or ingratitude. The contrary position — that God also responds to what the patriarchs and matriarchs and other saints did by favoring their descendants — is clearly spelled out as well, e.g., Abraham went and got a morsel of bread for the angels (Gen. 18:5), so God gave manna in the wilderness (Num. 11:8) and so on as a counterpart construction (T. Sot. 4:1–19). The same principle of divine reciprocity is expressed in connection with Deuteronomy 26:17–18, "You have declared this day concerning the Lord that he is your God." So, the passage goes on, "said the Holy One...to them, 'Just as you have made me the only object of your love in the world, so I shall make you the only object of my love in the world to come'" (T. Sot. 7:10C). This propositional statement does not convey the characterization of the one who said it, thus expressing the personal traits of God. It simply states, in yet another way, the basic thesis of Tosefta Sotah throughout, which is the prevalence of the principle of measure for measure in the fate of Israel. So too when there is heavenly communication in both the Mishnah and the Tosefta, it is ordinarily through the medium of a heavenly echo (e.g., T. Sot. 13:5ff.). God of course exacts punishment from the wicked and rewards the righteous (e.g., T. San. 8:3E).

If God is conceived as not merely a person but possessed of specific traits of personality, the Mishnah hardly contains evidence that its authorship could specify what those personal traits might be. True enough, one may infer from the rules that the Mishnah contains the attitudes of mind and preferences of personality of God as premise, who even is invoked as presence. For instance, God is assumed to favor deeds of lovingkindness and study of the Torah; honoring of parents; making peace among people. Accordingly, God may be assumed, as a personality, to be generous, studious, respectful, and irenic, a picture explicitly limned in tractate Avot. But no *stories* in particular portray God in one way rather than some other. No other modes of discourse, beside stories, portray God as a personality who in some vivid and concrete way embodies the desired virtues. God is not portrayed as a distinct and individual personality, walking, talking, caring, acting as people do. Once more, only when we examine such explicit portraits of the incarnation of God shall we understand the remarkable reticence of the Mishnah about the same matters.

True, we may impute such traits and others to the God who serves as premise and even presence. But the authorship of the Mishnah, unlike the diverse scriptural writers, simply did not portray God as a personality. Nor, apart from liturgical settings, is the fixed premise of God as giver of the Torah translated into the notion of the active presence of God in the everyday and the here and now. God hears and answers prayers of the individual — setting aside the general rules of being when God chooses to do so. The way in which another authorship among the canonical documents of the dual Torah portrays the personality of God will show us, in due course, what has not been done in the Mishnah. What we find in later documents, but not here, is a drastic shift in the modes of discourse concerning God.

In only one story in the entire Mishnah do I find a hint that God has a personality and therefore approaches the condition of incarnation in some concrete setting. Imputed to God is, specifically, a rather wry sense of humor. But the matter appears with remarkable subtlety, as we see in the account of how

Honi, the circle-drawer, in a rather childish way required God to give rain:

> On account of every sort of public trouble (may it not happen) do they sound the shofar, except for an excess of rain.
>
> They said to Honi, the circle drawer, "Pray for rain."
>
> He said to them, "Go and take in the clay ovens used for Passover, so that they not soften [in the rain which is coming]."
>
> He prayed, but it did not rain.
>
> What did he do?
>
> He drew a circle and stood in the middle of it and said before Him, "Lord of the world! Your children have turned to me, for before you I am like a member of the family. I swear by your great name — I'm simply not moving from here until you take pity on your children!"
>
> It began to rain drop by drop.
>
> He said, "This is not what I wanted, but rain for filling up cisterns, pits, and caverns."
>
> It began to rain violently.
>
> He said, "This is not what I wanted, but rain of good will, blessing, and graciousness."
>
> Now it rained the right way, until Israelites had to flee from Jerusalem up to the Temple Mount because of the rain.
>
> Now they came and said to him, "Just as you prayed for it to rain, now pray for it to go away."
>
> He said to them, "Go, see whether the stone of the strayers is disappeared."
>
> Simeon b. Shatah said to him, "If you were not Honi, I should decree a ban of excommunication against you. But what am I going to do to you? For you importune before the Omnipresent, so he does what you want, like a son who importunes his father, so he does what he wants. Concerning you Scripture says, Let your father and your mother be glad, and let her that bore you rejoice (Prov. 23:25)."

> M. Ta'anit 3:8

The picture in this very funny story of a rather petulant God, giving what was asked in such a way as to make fun of Honi, draws us near to a God with an interesting personality, no longer defined only by traits framed as rules, e.g., merciful and just, but now characterized as acting as the occasion required. Narrative in general finds more than slight place in the Mishnah, since the entire account of the Temple and its cult, the rites of the altar, the priesthood and their activities, is presented in essentially narrative form. But narrative never serves in the Mishnah as a vehicle for discussing the personality or activity of God.

Indeed, even when the opportunity to do so presents itself, the authorship of the Mishnah does not respond. The occasions that in Scripture commonly provoke God's anger — hence portraying God's personality in concrete terms — involve idolatry, which generates God's jealousy. The counterpart discourse in the Mishnah, Abodah Zarah, deals with worship of alien gods. No passage in that tractate refers to God's jealousy or anger with idols when Israelites worship idols. It is simply not a component of discourse on the subject. In the Mishnah's treatment of the matter, what is at stake is the relationship between Israelites and gentiles, not between Israel and God, and the purpose of the law is to define permissible and impermissible transactions with gentiles on the occasion of their celebration of their idol-gods. Secondary issues, e.g., use of foods prepared by gentiles, disposition of pieces of idols, and the like, do not change the picture of an authorship interested in outlining the boundaries between holy Israel and the gentile world. As in the Mishnah, so in the Tosefta, we find not a single story in which God is represented as a vivid personality.

The authorship of the Mishnah, like Israel in general, lived in a social world in which God formed a formidable presence everywhere. No wonder that the Mishnah's authorship found no necessity to restate on every possible occasion the premise of God's rule and authority. Quite to the contrary, in the course of setting forth the law only a few tractates explicitly refer to God, and most do not. The former classification of tractates, e.g., Berakhot, Ta'anit, involve liturgy, and the bulk of the explicit allusions to God — whether as premise or as person — appear quite naturally in discussion of prayer, with special attention to where, when, why, and above all how one says prayers (including blessings, supplications, thanksgiving, and the like). The latter tractates — nearly the whole of the Mishnah — implicitly refer to God when such topics as the proper conduct of rites on the various appointed seasons, the correct procedures of the sacrificial cult, the maintenance of the priesthood and the Temple, and the protection of the Temple from contamination come to the fore.

Accordingly, when we wish to hear how the Mishnah's authorship speaks of the premise of God's rule and presence, we may point to systematic statements of an implicit character: the divisions of Agriculture (maintaining the priesthood, giving God the share of the crop that is due to the divinity), Appointed Seasons (laws governing conduct on holy occasions, such as the Sabbath and festivals), Holy Things (rules for the conduct of the everyday rites of the Temple and for the upkeep of the building), and Purities (laws on uncleanness, beginning with those affecting the cult, as is specified in the book of Leviticus). We may further discover in the division of Women, governing family life, a very systematic expression of God's acute interest in matters of the sanctification of a woman's sexuality to a particular man, so that under some conditions sexual activity is punishable by heaven, while under others that same activity enjoys heaven's approval and blessing. Here too, in the exposition of the requirements of sanctification of the woman and sanctity of the family, I find implicit the premise of God's governance. Only the division of Damages fails to offer quite direct testimony to the same proposition, and even here we find numerous specific statements, e.g., M. San. 10:1ff., on the requirement, if one wishes to be (an) "Israel," of confessing that the resurrection of the dead constitutes a scripturally ordained truth. Statements of that order point toward the prevailing premise and permit us to claim quite simply that God as systemic premise is never far from the surface of the law of the Mishnah and, commonly, quite visible to the naked eye.

But that fact raises more questions than it settles. For it leads us to wonder how active a part God plays in the system of the Mishnah. Could the system of the Mishnah have taken shape without the premise of God? Certainly not. Does the system of the Mishnah, however, appeal to God, whether premise or presence, in the pursuit of solutions to its problems? Certainly not. And the exceptions to the rule are not only few but readily explained within the rules of the system, so hardly present exceptions at all. The focus of that system is on the discovery of the rules that govern a given classification of items — objects, facts, events — and (mostly in the secondary and exegetical work generated by the Mishnah) the harmonization of the prevailing rules with one another. The authorship of the Mishnah assigns to God, through the Torah, both priority and also a position of essential passivity, as a well-crafted legal system requires. For a God who intervenes violates the law. To the philosophers of the Mishnah, God guarantees the truth and regularity of the laws, deriving as they do from the Torah, but in particular cases God does not enforce those laws, nor should God have to. The very nature of the system prevents it. Allowing God under specified circumstances to hear and answer prayer need not, and does not, violate the orderly nature of the system, since the circumstances can be specified, and the required conditions met. So, in all, the emphasis on rules leaves God as the mere premise, not an active force in the system of the Mishnah.

Shall we then compare God to the laws of gravity? Once we recognize that God is an ubiquitous premise but never an independent variable, we see the aptness of such a metaphor. The laws of gravity, to a systematic account of the ecology of a botanical world, constitute a given and an immutable fact. Without those laws, it goes without saying, grass cannot sprout and trees cannot grow in the way in which they now do. But the laws of gravity, while necessary, are hardly sufficient — or, once conceded, even very urgent. They do not dictate many important systemic facts (though they make possible all facts) and they do not settle many of the system's interesting questions. So the laws of gravity in botany prove at once necessary and insufficient for explanation; implicit and ubiquitous, but not at all generative. Indeed, when we ask about the importance of the laws of gravity in a theory of botany — or biology, or plate tectonics in geology, for that matter — we see how awry matters have become. The laws are absolutely necessary but, even when sufficient, still not very interesting. And, to come to the worldview before us, we are therefore constrained to ask ourselves where is the God who acts? Where is the God who cares? Where is the God who rules "Israel" in accord with the Torah? In this system of philosophers with its law-abiding, philosophically acceptable God, the answer is: nowhere. Later on, in a system consequence to the Mishnah's, God would become not only necessary but also sufficient. Although without God the authorship of the Mishnah could not have constructed its system, for which God is necessary, still, since without God that authorship could have framed all of the system's most compelling propositions, God was hardly sufficient for the explanation of the system. God in the Mishnah's system is everywhere present, the ground of all being, giver and guarantor of the Torah — and a monumental irrelevance.

True, in any account of the Judaism "out there," beyond the pages of the Mishnah and yet presupposed and confessed by the authorship of the Mishnah, we must begin with God. Certainly, the worldview of the Mishnah takes shape around the datum of God's creation of the world and giving of the Torah. No one can imagine otherwise. But then that Judaism "out there" scarcely intersects with the profound concerns and urgent questions of the Judaism "in here," that is, the system of the Mishnah in particular. The Judaism "out there" turns out to make very little difference in the shaping and direction of the Judaism "in here," in the formation and structure of the worldview of the system at hand, and to contribute no more than the system-builders can utilize — if also no less.

2

Knowing God through the Torah: The Talmuds' God as Person

After the Mishnah, we come to its first and most important introduction, which is tractate Avot, a compilation that was concluded about a half century after the Mishnah, in ca. 250. That document's authorship strings together sayings of important authorities, from Sinai to one generation beyond the redaction of the Mishnah itself. The composition, called in English "the sayings of the founders," quite naturally rests upon the premises of the document it explains. But precisely how God appears in Avot is not to be predicted merely on that basis. It was at prayer that the authorship of tractate Avot encountered God as person, not merely as premise or even as presence. Still more generally, God as person cared for the sources of human action and distinguished proper from improper motivation. But what God does not do in the tractate is play an active part in the everyday encounter of sages and heaven. By that I mean that these sages did not report on God's discourse with them, what God said to them and what they said to God; they did not tell stories about God's doings.

The most important point made in tractate Abot is that our attitudes, emotions, sentiment, and intentionality should correspond to those of God:

> 2:4. He would say: Make His wishes into your own wishes, so that He will make your wishes into His wishes. Put aside your wishes on account of His wishes, so that He

44

will put aside the wishes of other people in favor of your wishes. Hillel says: Do not walk out on the community. And do not have confidence in yourself until the day you die. And do not judge your companion until you are in his place. And do not say anything which cannot be heard, for in the end it will be heard. And do not say: When I have time, I shall study, for you may never have time.

Serving "for the sake of heaven" finds its counterpart in another statement on right attitude. One should want what God wants, so that God will want what the person wants. This is immediately qualified: one should accede to God's wishes over one's own desires, which will provoke a counterpart action in heaven. Here God finds representation as, if not a personality, then a person, with wishes that respond to those of the human being. Here is the first clear representation of incarnation. We are like God because God's feelings and emotions and desires correspond to those of humanity. One's duty, then, is to subordinate one's feelings and desires to those of God, conceived once more as the master to whom everyone relates as subordinate — but who then will respond to the will and wishes of subordinates of appropriate demeanor and conduct.

But while we may be like God, we are not equivalent or counterpart. We are always human and mortal; God is always supernatural and immortal:

> 3:1A. Aqabiah b. Mehallalel says, "Reflect upon three things and you will not fall into the clutches of transgression: "Know (1) from whence you come, (2) whither you are going, and (3) before whom you are going to have to give a full account of yourself.
>
> 3:1B. "From whence do you come? From a putrid drop. Whither are you going? To a place of dust, worms, and maggots.
>
> 3:1C. "And before whom are you are going to give a full account of yourself? Before the King of kings of kings, the Holy One, blessed be he."

We come from nowhere, we go to death, we give our account before the heavenly King, God on high. The familiar attitude that before God as person one gives a full account found a ready hearing among the authors of the Mishnah. The important thing is once more the linking of God as person to the correct attitude toward God as person.

Now we find Torah study treated as the Mishnah treats prayer. The attitudes required for the one are now demanded for the other. The broadening of the personhood of God takes place in this movement outward from words of prayer to words of Torah study. Study is treated as counterpart to praying, a position not suggested by the authorship of the Mishnah.

> 3:3. R. Simeon says, Three who ate at a single table and did not talk about teachings of the Torah while at that table are as though they ate from dead sacrifices (Ps. 106:28), as it is said, "For all tables are full of vomit and filthiness [if they are] without God" (Ps. 106:28). But three who ate at a single table and did talk about teachings of the Torah while at that table are as if they ate at the table of the Omnipresent, blessed is he, as it is said, "And he said to me, This is the table that is before the Lord" (Ezek. 41:22)."

The point is the same as before, equally explicit and fresh.

> 3:4. R. Hananiah b. Hakhinai says, (1) he who gets up at night, and (2) he who walks around by himself, and (3) he who turns his desire to emptiness — lo, this person is liable for his life.
>
> 3:5. R. Nehunia b. Haqqaneh says, From whoever accepts upon himself the yoke of the Torah do they remove the yoke of the state and the yoke of hard labor. And upon whoever removes from himself the yoke of the Torah do they lay the yoke of the state and the yoke of hard labor.
>
> 3:6. R. Halafta of Kefar Hananiah says, Among ten who sit and work hard on the Torah the Presence comes to rest, as it is said, "God stands in the congregation of God" (Ps. 82:1). And how do we know that the same is so even of five? For it is said, "And he has founded his group upon the earth" (Amos 9:6). And how do we know that this is so even of three? Since it is said, "And he judges among the judges" (Ps. 82:1). And how do we know that this is

so even of two? Because it is said, "Then they that feared the Lord spoke with one another, and the Lord hearkened and heard" (Mal. 3:16). And how do we know that this is so even of one? Since it is said, "In every place where I record my name I will come to you and I will bless you" (Exod. 20:24).

The shift from prayer to Torah study accounts for the striking allegation that God is present among all those who engage in Torah study. God is encountered as person in the Torah as much as in prayer, and this point is repeated time and again. Obviously, to these allegations God is critical. But God does not require extensive description; the person remains essentially premise, but the generative inquiry attends to other matters, particularly Torah study. Tractate Avot works out its sayings mainly on the twin themes of study through discipleship and application of the Torah, which serves as a handbook for disciples. To that program God is of course necessary, but, with regard to making the points the authorship wishes to register, also insufficient. God is not represented as a sage; God is not portrayed as the model for the disciple or master; and God is not set forth as a student of the Torah. These later motifs never enter the imagination of our authorship. To state the matter very simply, God, now seen as the model and likeness by which the human emotions and attitudes take their measure, has yet to undergo that stage of metaphorization that renders God incarnate. To state matters as our sages would, we are like God in our right attitudes, and God responds, therefore, to our desires and feelings; but we are not like God in our very being, our shape and form, our activity and concrete life.

The principal motif in the Judaic account of God is that God loves humanity and shows infinite mercy and patience toward humanity; and the sign of God's love is the giving of the Torah, which informs humanity of the truth concerning its standing, "in our image, after our likeness":

> 3:14A. He would say, Precious is the human being, who was created in the image [of God]. It was an act of still greater love that it was made known to him that he was

created in the image [of God]. As it is said, "For in the image of God he made man" (Gen. 9:6).

3:14B. Precious are Israelites, who are called children to the Omnipresent. It was an act of still greater love that it was made known to them that they were called children to the Omnipresent, as it is said, "You are the children of the Lord your God" (Deut. 14:1).

3:14C. Precious are Israelites, to whom was given the precious thing. It was an act of still greater love that it was made known to them that to them was given that precious thing with which the world was made, as it is said, "For I give you a good doctrine. Do not forsake my Torah" (Prov. 4:2).

God's love — like the love of a human being — takes form in God's informing humanity, in particular Israel, of that love. Once more God is given personhood, with traits remarkably like those of the human being who forms the model or the ideal of our authorship. The step yet to be taken will turn the shared psychological traits into a common incarnate being, God as not merely presence but engaged personality. One step remains, that is, the description of God in the concrete terms in which one describes a personality. That would be taken in the next major collection of writings.

Beyond the Mishnah and tractate Abot come the Talmud of the Land of Israel, or Yerushalmi, generally supposed to have come to a conclusion at ca. 400 C.E.; Genesis Rabbah, assigned to about the next half century; Leviticus Rabbah, ca. 450 C.E.; Pesiqta deRab Kahana, ca. 450–500 C.E.; and, finally, the Talmud of Babylonia, or Bavli, assigned to the late sixth or early seventh century, ca. 600 C.E. The two Talmuds systematically interpret passages of the Mishnah, and the other documents the same for books of the written Torah. These sages portray what it means to know God "in our image, after our likeness" in a stunning account:

> Said R. Hoshaiah, "When the Holy One, blessed be he, came to create the first man, the ministering angels mistook him [for God, since man was in God's image,] and

wanted to say before him, 'Holy, [holy, holy is the Lord of hosts].'

"To what may the matter be compared? To the case of a king and a governor who were set in a chariot, and the provincials wanted to greet the king, 'Sovereign!' But they did not know which one of them was which. What did the king do? He turned the governor out and put him away from the chariot, so that people would know who was king.

"So too when the Holy One, blessed be he, created the first man, the angels mistook him [for God]. What did the Holy One, blessed be he, do? He put him to sleep, so everyone knew that he was a mere man.

"That is in line with the following verse of Scripture: 'Cease you from man, in whose nostrils is a breath, for how little is he to be accounted'" (Isa. 2:22).

Genesis Rabbah VIII:X.

Accordingly, our sages saw God enthroned, riding horses or chariots. Not only so, but given the exegesis of the Song of Songs as a love song between God and Israel, on which basis that book found its way into the canon of Judaism, we must suppose many accepted the interpretation. God, not as premise but as immediate presence, does not very often play an everyday and active role in the Mishnah's processes and system of decision-making. The contrast between God as essentially a premise of all being and God as an active personality engaged in everyday transactions with specific persons comes to full expression in the passage at hand.

In the following passage, God serves as the origin of all great teachings, but as we have seen, that fact bears no consequences for the description of God as a person or personality:

E. "Given by one shepherd" —

F. Said the Holy One, blessed be he, "If you hear a teaching from an Israelite minor, and it gave pleasure to you, let it not be in your sight as if one has heard it from a minor, but as if one has heard it from an adult,

G. "and let it not be as if one has heard it from an adult, but as if one has heard it from a sage,

H. "and let it not be as if one has heard it from a sage,
but as if one has heard it from a prophet,

I. "and let it not be as if one has heard it from a prophet,
but as if one has heard it from the shepherd,

J. "and there is as a shepherd only Moses, in line with
the following passage: 'Then he remembered the days of
old, of Moses his servant. Where is he who brought out of
the sea the shepherds of his flock? Where is he who put in
the midst of them his holy Spirit?' " (Isa. 63:11).

K. "It is not as if one has heard it from the shepherd but
as if one has heard it from the Almighty."

L. "Given by one Shepherd" — and there is only One
who is the Holy One, blessed be he, in line with that which
you read in Scripture: "Hear, O Israel: the Lord our God is
one Lord" (Deut. 6:4).

Y. San. 10:1.IX

In studying the Torah, sages and disciples clearly met the living
God and recorded a direct encounter with and experience of
God through the revealed word of God. But in a statement such
as this, alluding to, but not clearly describing, what it means to
hear the word of the Almighty, God at the end of the line simply forms the premise of revelation. There is no further effort at
characterization. The exposition of the work of creation (Y. Hag.
2:1.IIff.) refers to God's deeds, mainly by citing verses of Scripture, e.g., "Then he made the snow: 'He casts forth his ice like
morsels' " (Ps. 147:17), and so on. So too God has wants and
desires, e.g., what God wants is for Israel to repent, at which
time God will save Israel (Y. Ta. 1:1X.U), but there is no effort
to characterize God.

When actions are attributed to God, we have of course to recognize God's presence in context, e.g., "The Holy One, blessed
be he, kept to himself [and did not announce] the reward that
is coming to those who carry out their religious duties, so that
they should do them in true faith [without expecting a reward]"
(Y. Qid. 1:7.IX.B). But such a statement hardly constitutes evidence that God is present and active in a given circumstance.
It rather forms into a personal statement the principle that one
should do religious duties for the right motive, not expecting

a reward — a view we found commonplace in tractate Avot. So too statements of God's action carry slight characterization, e.g., "Even if 999 aspects of the argument of an angel incline against someone, but a single aspect of the case of that angel argues in favor, the Holy One . . . still inclines the scales in favor of the accused" (Y. Qid. i:9.II.S). It remains to observe that when we find in the Yerushalmi a sizable narrative of intensely important events, such as the destruction of Betar in the time of Bar Kokhba (Y. Ta. 4:5.Xff.), God scarcely appears except, again, as premise and source of all that happens. There is no characterization, nor even the claim that God intervened in some direct and immediate way, though I do not believe we can imagine anyone thought otherwise. That simple affirmation reaches expression, for instance, in this observation in connection with the destruction of the Temple: "It appears that the Holy One, blessed be he, wants to exact from our hand vengeance for his blood" (Y. Ta. 4:5.XIV.Q). That sort of intrusion hardly suggests a vivid presence of God as part of the narrative scheme, let alone a characterization of God as person.

Sages in the Yerushalmi may have made up conversations between biblical heroes and God, but when it came to their own day, such conversations took the form of prayers. As to the former:

> At that very moment, David said to the Holy One, blessed be he, "Master of the Universe, shall your presence descend upon the earth? May your presence rise up from among them! . . . " [David is urging God to remain over the earth and not among gossip-mongers on earth.]
> Y. Pe. 1:1.XXV.C (trans. Roger Brooks)

In this case, a conversation between God and David is made up; I cannot point in the Yerushalmi to equivalent conversations involving sages.

But of course God does occur as a "you" throughout the Yerushalmi, most commonly, of course, in a liturgical setting. As in the earlier documents of the oral part of the Torah, so in the Yerushalmi we have a broad range of prayers to God as "you," illustrated by the following.

> R. Ba bar Zabeda in the name of Rab: "[The congrega-
> tion says this prayer in an undertone:] 'We give thanks to
> you, for we must praise your name. My lips will shout for
> joy when I sing praises to you, my soul also which you
> have rescued (Ps. 71:23). Blessed are you, Lord, God of
> praises.' "
>
> Y. Ber. 1:4.VIII.D (trans. Tzvee Zahavy)

Since the formula of the blessing invokes "you," we find nothing
surprising in the liturgical person imagined by the framers of
various prayers. God's ad hoc intervention as an active and par-
ticipating personality in specific situations is treated as more
or less a formality, in that the rules are given and will come
into play without ordinarily requiring God to join in a given
transaction:

> When one enters the study hall, what does he say? "May
> it be your will, Lord my God, God of my fathers, that I
> shall not be angry with my colleagues and they not be
> angry with me; that we not declare what is clean to be
> unclean and vice versa; that we not declare what is per-
> mitted to be forbidden and vice versa; lest I find myself
> put to shame in this world and in the world to come."
>
> Y. Ber. 4:2.I.Aff. (trans. Tzvee Zahavy)

Here we see yet another fine instance in which God is a "you,"
but in which that "you" does not intervene in a particular case
or engage in a concrete ad hoc transaction. "May it be your
will, . . . " a standard liturgical formula, never is followed by a
tale showing how, on a specific occasion, the divine will (or the
opposite) was expressed.

God was encountered as a very real presence, actively listen-
ing to prayers, as in the following:

> See how high the Holy One, blessed be he, is above
> his world. Yet a person can enter a synagogue, stand be-
> hind a pillar, and pray in an undertone, and the Holy One,
> blessed be he, hears his prayers, as it says, "Hannah was
> speaking in her heart; only her lips moved, and her voice

was not heard" (1 Sam. 1:13). Yet the Holy One, blessed be
he, heard her prayer.

Y. Ber. 9:1.VII.E

When, however, we distinguish God as person, "you," from
God as a well-portrayed active personality, liturgical formulas give a fine instance of the one side of the distinction. In
the Yerushalmi's sizable corpus of such prayers, individual and
community alike, we never find testimony to a material change
in God's decision in a case based on setting aside known
rules in favor of an episodic act of intervention. It follows that
thought on God as person remains continuous with what has
gone before. Sages, like everyone else in Israel, believed that
God hears and answers prayer. But that belief did not require
them to preserve stories about specific instances in which the
rules of hearing and answering prayer attested to a particular trait of personality or character to be imputed to God. A
specific episode or incident never served to highlight the characterization of divinity in one way rather than in some other,
in a manner parallel to Scripture authorships' use of stories to
portray God as a sharply etched personality.

For yet another example of God as person in a liturgical
passage, Y. Ta. 2:1I.G–H (among many instances) uses the imperative: "[They sound the horns] as if to say, 'Consider us as
if we cry like a beast before you.' " But in the personification of
God, referred to in context as "Lord of the world," we find very
few sustained conversations in which God takes an active role
in discourse. An example of the essentially passive character of
God as "you" is in the following:

> R. Simeon b. Yohai taught, "The book of Deuteronomy
> went up and spread itself out before the Holy One, blessed
> be he, saying before him, 'Lord of the world! You have
> written in your Torah that any covenant, part of which is
> null is wholly nullified. Now lo, Solomon wishes to up-
> root a Y of mine.' Said to him the Holy One, blessed be
> he, 'Solomon and a thousand like him will be null, but not
> one word of yours will be nullified.' "

Y. San. 2:6.II.AA–DD

As commonly is the case, here the depiction of God follows the logic of the story. God has no particular traits imputed by the narrative, rather serving as a conversation partner for the book of Deuteronomy. Still, God is portrayed as a person, not merely a presence.

One aspect of personhood is capacity to carry out deeds, and, it goes without saying, in the document at hand God is represented as doing things, past, present, and future, for example:

> R. Berekhiah in the name of R. Abba bar Kahan: "In the future, the Holy One, blessed be he, is going to set the place of the righteous closer to his throne than the place of the ministering angels. The ministering angels will ask them and say to them, 'What has God wrought?' (Num. 23:23). That is, what did the Holy One, blessed be he, teach you?"
>
> Said R. Levi bar Hayyuta, "Did he not do so in this world? . . . "
>
> Y. Shab. 6:9.II.HH–II

God's doing this or that forms part of a larger portrait of God as a person capable of carrying out purposive deeds. When, presently, we meet God as a fully etched personality, God will be shown to do the deeds human beings do in the way that human beings do them. At this point, by contrast, even a very long catalogue of the great deeds of God cannot yield much of a picture of God as a "you," a person people may know and love.

Not only so, but the representation in the Yerushalmi of God as a person does not fully work out the potential invited by a given subject. For example, God is angry — so Scripture says — on account of idolatry. Yet in the Yerushalmi's exposition of the pertinent chapters of Abodah Zarah, chapters 3ff., I find not a single story of God's anger embodied in a picture of God as a person, let alone as a personality. The matter is left as a prevailing attitude or principle. When God does appear, it is as an essentially passive participant, e.g., the conversation partner who asks, "Why?" or who confirms what the protagonist proposes, as in the following:

I. But the Holy One, blessed be he, said to Elijah, "This Hiel is a great man. Go and see him [because his sons have died]."

J. He said to him, "I am not going to see him."

K. He said to him, "Why?"

L. He said to him, "For if I go and they say things which will outrage you, I shall not be able to bear it."

M. He said to him, "Then if they say things which outrage me, whatever you decree against them I shall carry out."

Y. San. 10:2.III

Here God is person and not abstract principle or premise, but not a vividly etched personality. The conversation consists of an exchange of conventional theological positions, not a transaction between two distinctive personalities, each entering into a one-time exchange with the other. Another example of the same phenomenon is as follows:

O. It is written, "Then the word of the Lord came to Isaiah: 'Go and say to Hezekiah, Thus says the Lord, the God of David your father: I have heard your prayer, I have seen your tears; behold I will add fifteen years to your life'" (Isa. 38:4–5).

P. [Isaiah] said to him, "Thus I've already told him, and how thus do I say to him?

Q. "He is a man occupied with great affairs, and he will not believe me."

R. [God] said to him, "He is a very humble man, and he will believe you. And not only so, but as yet the rumor has not yet gone forth in the city."

S. "And before Isaiah had gone out of the middle court, [the word of the Lord came to him]" (2 Kings 20:4).

Y. San. 10:2.VI

Here once again God is a mere conversation partner, a straight man once more, pointing to facts already established in context and doing nothing more than moving the narrative along by word or deed. When God serves as the protagonist of a story and leads the conversation and when God's part in the conversation is particular to that context and not simply the proclamation of well-known theological principles, then we shall meet God as a fully spelled out and individual personality: divinity in the form of humanity. But it is not in the present compilation, so far as I have been able to discover. Yet another case is in the same context:

> Q. Now all the ministering angels went and closed the windows, so that the prayer of Manasseh should not reach upward to the Holy One, blessed be he.
> R. The ministering angels were saying before the Holy One, blessed be he, "Lord of the world, a man who worshiped idols and put up an image in the Temple — are you going to accept him back as a penitent?"
> S. He said to them, "If I do not accept him back as a penitent, lo, I shall lock the door before all penitents."
> T. What did the Holy One, blessed be he, do? He made an opening [through the heavens] under his throne of glory and listened to his supplication.
> U. That is in line with the following verse of Scripture: "He prayed to him, and God received his entreaty ('TR) and heard his supplication and brought him again [to Jerusalem into his kingdom]. [Then Manasseh knew that the Lord was God]" (2 Chron. 33:13).
>
> Y. San. 10:2.VII

Here we have a more concrete characterization of a deed done by God, which shows God's character as merciful. Yet another passage that shows the same tendency is as follows:

> Said R. Phineas, " 'Good and upright is the Lord. Therefore he instructs sinners in the way' (Ps. 25:8). Why is he good? Because he is upright. And why upright? Because he is good. 'Therefore he instructs sinners in the way' by teaching them the way to repentance."
> They asked Wisdom, "As to a sinner, what is his punishment?"
> She said to them, "Evil pursues the evil" (Prov. 13:21).
> They asked prophecy, "As to a sinner, what is his punishment?"

> She said to them, "The soul that sins shall die" (Ezek. 18:20).
>
> They asked the Holy One, blessed be he, "As to a sinner, what is his punishment?"
>
> He said to them, "Let the sinner repent, and his sin will be forgiven for him, as it is said, 'Therefore he instructs sinners in the way' (Ps. 25:8). He shows sinners the way to repentance."
>
> Y. Mak. 2:6.IV

This is a further excellent example of how God as person represents a mere hypostatization, without concrete and particular traits. When God is represented as a "you," it turns out (thus far) to form a mere formality of rhetoric.

Imputing thoughts or public statements to God therefore does not much change the picture, as in the following:

> Said R. Levi, "What is the meaning of slow to 'anger'?
>
> "The matter may be compared to a king who had two tough legions. He said, 'If they live here with me in the capital, if the city folk anger me, they will immediately put them down with brute force. I shall send them a long way away, so that if the city folk anger me, while I am yet summoning the legions, the people will appease me and I shall accept their plea.'
>
> "Likewise, the Holy One, blessed be he, said, 'Anger and wrath are angels of destruction. Lo, I shall send them a long way away, and if Israel angers me, while I am summoning and bringing them to me, Israel will repent and I shall accept their repentance.' "
>
> Y. Ta. 2:1.XI.I–K

God may further serve as an active voice, but only in the paraphrase of an available verse of Scripture, as in the following:

> Said R. Judah b. Pazzi, "[God said,] 'That [dew] which I gave as a bequest which may be nullified to Abraham, I give [to his descendants as a gift which can never be nullified], "May God give you of the dew of heaven" (Gen. 27:28.)' "
>
> Y. Ber. 5:2.I.D

Here we have assigned to God simply an amplification of the cited verse of Scripture. Yet another case in which God speaks without emerging as a well-etched personality is the following:

> Said R. Samuel bar Nahman, "Said the Holy One, blessed be he, to David, 'David, I shall count out for you a full complement of days. I shall not give you less than the full number. Will Solomon, your son, not build the Temple in order to offer sacrifices in it? But more precious to me are the just and righteous deeds which you do than the offerings which will be made in the Temple'"
>
> Y. Sheq. 2:6.VI.D

Numerous examples will not vastly change the picture. God is represented as a person, but not as much of a personality. God's rulings, rather than God's attitudes or emotions or deeds in a concrete narrative, are simply restated in dialogue form. That establishes God as a person, but does not then provide a rich characterization at all.

While God makes a statement in the first person, in fact it is nothing more than a restatement of the point of the parable and does not, therefore, constitute a characterization of God in some particular framework. If the storyteller had spoken in the third person, that is, instead of using "I" using simply "the Holy One," in no way would the course of the story have shifted. The point of the story lies in imputing to the divinity the trait of patience, not in describing a patient personality in some particular framework. Moreover, even when parables are drawn, they commonly illustrate principles or traits rather than serving to characterize a highly individual personality. For example, in the following parable, God is shown to be more loyal as a patron than a human counterpart. But this turns out merely to illustrate a point Scripture has made and hardly serves to express in words a vivid personality:

> R. Yudan in the name of R. Isaac gave four discourses: "A person had a human patron. One day they came and told the patron, 'A member of your household has been arrested.'
>
> "He said to them, 'Let me take his place.'

"They said to him, 'Lo, he is already going out to trial.'
"He said to them, 'Let me take his place.'
"They said to him, 'Lo, he is going to be hanged.'
"Now where is he, and where his patron?
"But the Holy One, blessed be he, [will save his subjects just as he] saved Moses from the sword of Pharaoh. This is in accord with what is written, 'He delivered me from the sword of Pharaoh' " (Exod. 18:4).
                    Y. Ber. 9:1.VIII.B–C (trans. Tzvee Zahavy)

The passage goes through a sequence of examples of the same fact deriving from Scripture, namely, God's personal salvation of the saints. God is further portrayed as loyal and humble, identifying with Israel even in their poverty, ignorance, and humiliation (Y. Ber. 9:1.XI, for one important example). But at no point in the exposition do we find either an immediate case, deriving from sages' own time, or, more to the point, a clear characterization of God in specific and vivid terms. God acts, as Scripture has made clear, and evidence of God's will and person all derive from Scripture. For instance, while everyone believed God answers prayers, where evidence of that fact is adduced, it is from Scripture's cases:

Said R. Judah b. Pazzi, "Even if a woman in labor is already seated in the delivery chair, God can change the sex of the foetus, in accord with the verse, 'Behold like clay in the hand of the potter, so you are in my hand, O house of Israel' " (Jer. 18:6).
Rabbi in the name of the house of Yannai: "Originally Dinah was a male. After Rachel prayed, she was changed into a female. So it says, 'Afterwards she bore a daughter and called her Dinah' (Gen. 30:21). It was after Rachel prayed that Dinah was changed into a female."
                    Y. Ber. 9:3.VI.B–C (trans. Tzvee Zahavy)

The evidence is then expounded wholly within the framework of principles established by biblical facts, without a further effort to transform these facts into the portrait of a living personality. God emerges as a person, vital and alive in the life of

Israel, but in no way incarnate in everyday encounters, stories of a personality people might know and engage in conversation.

Telling stories — as in Hasidism later on — provides the particular means by which theological traits that long generations had affirmed now are portrayed as qualities of the personality of God, who is like a human being. It is one thing to hypostatize a theological abstraction, e.g., "The quality of mercy said before the Holy One, blessed be he...." It is quite another to construct a conversation between God and, e.g., David, with a complete argument and a rich interchange, in which God's merciful character is spelled out as the trait of a specific personality. And that is what we find in the Bavli and, so far as my survey suggests, not in any prior document.

Specifically, it is in the Bavli, the second and final Talmud, that the specification of an attribute of God, such as long-suffering, is restated by means of narrative. God then emerges not as an abstract entity with theological traits but as a fully exposed personality. God is portrayed as engaged in conversation with human beings because God and humanity can understand one another within the same rules of discourse. When we speak of the personality of God, we shall see, traits of a corporeal, emotional, and social character form the repertoire of appropriate characteristics. To begin with, we consider the particular means by which, in the pages of the Talmud of Babylonia, or Bavli, in particular, these traits are set forth.

The following story shows us the movement from the abstract and theological to the concrete and narrative mode of discourse about God:

> "And Moses made haste and bowed his head toward the earth and worshiped" (Exod. 34:8):
>
> What did Moses see?
>
> R. Haninah b. Gamula said, "He saw [God's attribute of] being long-suffering [Exod. 34:7]."
>
> Rabbis say, "He saw [the attribute of] truth [Exod. 34:7].
>
> "It has been taught on Tannaite authority in accord with him who has said, "He saw God's attribute of being long-suffering."
>
> For it has been taught on Tannaite authority:

> When Moses went up on high, he found the Holy One,
> blessed be he, sitting and writing, "Long-suffering."
> He said before him, "Lord of the world, long-suffering
> for the righteous?"
> He said to him, "Also for the wicked."
> [Moses] said to him, "Let the wicked perish."
> He said to him, "Now you will see what you want."
> When the Israelites sinned, he said to him, "Did I not
> say to you, 'Long suffering for the righteous'?"
> He said to him, "Lord of the world, did I not say to you,
> 'Also for the wicked'?"
> That is in line with what is written, "And now I beseech
> you, let the power of my Lord be great, according as you
> have spoken, saying" (Num. 14:17). [Freedman, *The Babylo-*
> *nian Talmud: Sanhedrin,* 764, n. 7: What called forth Moses'
> worship of God when Israel sinned through the Golden
> Calf was his vision of the Almighty as long-suffering.]
>   B. San 111a–b, VI

The statement at the outset is repeated in narrative form at Fff.
Once we are told that God is long-suffering, then it is in particular, narrative form that that trait is given definition. God then
emerges as a personality, specifically because Moses engages in
argument with God. He reproaches God, questions God's actions and judgments, holds God to a standard of consistency —
and receives appropriate responses. God in heaven does not argue with humanity on earth. God in heaven issues decrees,
forms the premise of the earthly rules, constitutes a presence,
may even take the form of a "you" for hearing and answering
prayers.

When God argues, discusses, defends, and explains actions,
emerges as a personality described in words, then God attains
that personality that imparts to God the status of a being consubstantial with humanity. It is in particular through narrative
that that transformation of God from person to personality
takes place. Since personality, as I have defined the term, involves physical traits, attitudes of mind, emotion, and intellect
consubstantial with those of human beings, and the doing of
the deeds people do in the way in which they do them, I have

now to demonstrate that all three modes of personality come to full expression in the Bavli. This we do in sequence, ending with a clear demonstration that God incarnate takes the particular form of a sage. And that will yield the problem of the final chapter, namely, the difference between God and all (other) sages.

The claim that the character of God is shaped in the model of a human being requires substantiation, first of all, in quite physical traits, such as are taken for granted in the passage just now cited. Incarnation means precisely that: representation of God in the flesh, as a human being, in the present context, as a man. We begin with a clear statement that has God represented as a man, seen in the interpretation of the vision of the prophet Zechariah:

> And said R. Yohanan, "What is the meaning of the verse of Scripture, 'I saw by night, and behold a man riding upon a red horse, and he stood among the myrtle trees that were in the bottom' " (Zech. 1:8)
>
> "What is the meaning of, 'I saw by night'?
>
> "The Holy One, blessed be he, sought to turn the entire world into night.
>
> " 'And behold, a man riding' — 'man' refers only to the Holy One, blessed be he, as it is said, 'The Lord is a man of war, the Lord is his name' (Exod. 15:3).
>
> " 'On a red horse' — the Holy One, blessed be he, sought to turn the entire world to blood.
>
> "When, however, he saw Hananiah, Mishael, and Azariah, he cooled off, as it is said, 'And he stood among the myrtle trees that were in the deep.' "
>
> B. Sanhedrin 1:1.XLII [93A]

We recall the explicit statement in this same regard:

> [It was necessary for] the Holy One, blessed be he, to say to them, "You see me in many forms. But I am the same one who was at the sea, I am the same one who was at Sinai, *I [anokhi] am the Lord your God who brought you out of the land of Egypt*" (Exod. 20:2).

Scripture of course knows that God has a face, upon which human beings are not permitted to gaze. But was that face understood in a physical way, and did God enjoy other physical characteristics? An affirmative answer emerges clearly in the following:

"And he said, 'You cannot see my face'" (Exod. 33:20).
It was taught on Tannaite authority in the name of R. Joshua b. Qorha, "This is what the Holy One, blessed be he, said to Moses:

"'When I wanted [you to see my face], you did not want to, now that you want to see my face, I do not want you to.'"

This differs from what R. Samuel bar Nahmani said that R. Jonathan said.

For R. Samuel bar Nahmani said that R. Jonathan said, "As a reward for three things he received the merit of three things.

"As a reward for: 'And Moses hid his face' (Exod. 3:6), he had the merit of having a glistening face.

"As a reward for: 'Because he was afraid to' (Exod. 3:6), he had the merit that 'They were afraid to come near him' (Exod. 34:30).

"As a reward for: 'To look upon God' (Exod. 3:6), he had the merit: 'The similitude of the Lord does he behold'" (Num. 12:8).

"And I shall remove my hand and you shall see my back" (Exod. 33:23).

R. Hana bar Bizna said that R. Simeon the Pious said, "This teaches that the Holy One, blessed be he, showed Moses [how to tie] the knot of the phylacteries."

b Ber. 7A, LVI.

That God is able to tie the knot indicates that God has fingers and other physical gifts. God furthermore is portrayed as wearing phylacteries as well. It follows that God has an arm and a forehead. There is no element of a figurative reading of the indicated traits. That is why, when God is further represented as having eyes and teeth, we have no reason to assign that picture to the status of mere poetry:

"His eyes shall be red with wine, and his teeth white
with milk" (Gen. 49:12):

R. Dimi, when he came, interpreted the verse in this
way: "The congregation of Israel said to the Holy One,
blessed be he, 'Lord of the Universe, wink to me with your
eyes, which gesture will be sweeter than wine, and show
me your teeth, which gesture will be sweeter than milk.'"

b Ket. 111b

The attribution of physical traits is explicit and no longer general or possibly figurative. Another such representation assigns
to God cheeks:

Said R. Joshua b. Levi, "What is the meaning of the
following verse of Scripture: 'His cheeks are as a bed of
spices' (Song 5:13)?

"From every word that came forth from the mouth of
the Holy One, blessed be he, the world was filled with the
fragrance of spices.

"But since, by the first word, the world was filled, where
did the fragrance of the second go?

"The Holy One, blessed be he, brought forth wind from
his treasury and made each pass in sequence: 'His lips are
as lilies dripping myrrh that passes on' (Song 5:13) — read
the word for lilies as though it yielded the sense 'that lead
step by step.'"

b Shab. 88b

From eyes and teeth and cheeks, we move on to the physical attributes of having limbs. In the following passage, God is given
hands and palms:

Further, [the congregation of Israel] made its request in
an improper manner, "O God, set me as a seal on your
heart, as a seal on your arm" (Song 8:6).

[But the Holy One, blessed be he, responded in a proper
way.] Said the Holy One, blessed be he, to [the congregation of Israel,] "My daughter, now you are asking for
something which sometimes can be seen and sometimes
cannot be seen. But I shall give you something which can
always be seen.

"For it is said, 'Behold, I have graven you on the palms of my hands' (Isa. 49:16) [and the palms are always visible, in a way in which the heart and arm are not]."

b Ta. 4a

Hands are attached to arms, and it is implicit that God has arms as well. That God has arms again is shown by the claim that God puts on phylacteries just as Moses does:

R. Abin bar Ada said that R. Isaac said, "How do we know on the basis of Scripture that the Holy One, blessed be he, puts on phylacteries? As it is said, 'The Lord has sworn by his right hand, and by the arm of his strength' (Isa. 62:8).

" 'By his right hand' refers to Torah, as it is said, 'At his right hand was a fiery law for them' (Deut. 33:2).

" 'And by the arm of his strength' refers to phylacteries, as it is said, 'The Lord will give strength to his people' (Ps. 29:11).

"And how do we know that phylacteries are a strength for Israel? For it is written, 'And all the peoples of the earth shall see that the name of the Lord is called upon you and they shall be afraid of you' " (Deut. 28:10).

And it has been taught on Tannaite authority:

R. Eliezer the Great says, "This [Deut. 28:10] refers to the phylacteries that are put on the head."

b Ber. 6A, XXXVIII

Once more we find very clear evidence of a corporeal conception of God. We have no basis on which to assume the authorship at hand meant a merely poetic characterization or, indeed, what a more spiritual interpretation would have required. Assuming that the words mean precisely what they say, we have to conclude that God is here portrayed as incarnate. Later on we shall be told what passages of Scripture are written in the phylacteries that God puts onto his right arm and forehead.

We shall presently review the range of God's emotions, which appear to be much the same as human ones. But first let us skip on to the matter of God's doing what people do, in the way in which they do it. In the Bavli's stories God not only looks like a human being but also performs the acts that human beings do. For example, God spends the day in much the same way as a mortal ruler of Israel, at least as sages imagine such a figure. That is, he studies the Torah, makes practical decisions, and sustains the world (meaning that God administers public funds for public needs) — just as sages do (in the sages' picture of themselves). A deeply human God is depicted in the final part of the day when God plays with his pet leviathan. Some correct that view and hold that God spends the rest of the day teaching youngers. In passages such as these we therefore see the concrete expression of the personality of God:

> R. Judah said that Rab said, "The day is twelve hours long. During the first three, the Holy One, blessed be he, is engaged in the study of the Torah.
>
> "During the next three God sits in judgment on the world and when he sees the world sufficiently guilty to deserve destruction, he moves from the seat of justice to the seat of mercy.
>
> "During the third he feeds the whole world, from the horned buffalo to vermin.
>
> "During the fourth he plays with the leviathan, as it is said, 'There is leviathan, whom you have made to play with' " (Ps. 104:26).
>
> [Another authority denies this final point and says,] "What then does God do in the fourth quarter of the day?"
>
> "He sits and teaches school children, as it is said, 'Whom shall one teach knowledge, and whom shall one make to understand the message? Those who are weaned from milk' " (Isa. 28:9).
>
> And what does God do by night?
>
> If you like, I shall propose that he does what he does in daytime.
>
> Or if you prefer: he rides a light cherub and floats in eighteen thousand worlds....
>
> Or if you prefer: he sits and listens to the song of the heavenly creatures, as it is said, "By the day the Lord will

command his lovingkindness and in the night his song shall be with me" (Ps. 42:9).

b A.Z. 3b

Other actions of God that presuppose a physical capacity are indicated in the following, although the picture is not so clearly one of concrete physical actions as in the earlier instances:

R. Judah said that Rab said, "Everything that Abraham personally did for the ministering angels the Holy One, blessed be he, personally did for his children, and everything that Abraham did through servants the Holy One, blessed be he, carried out also through ministering angels.

" 'And Abraham ran to the herd' (Gen. 18:7). 'And a wind went forth from the Lord' (Num. 11:31).

" 'And he took butter and milk' (Gen. 18:8). 'Behold, I will rain bread from heaven for you' (Exod. 16:4).

" 'And he stood by them under the tree' (Gen. 18:8). 'Behold, I will stand before you there upon the rock' " (Exod. 17:6).

B. B.M. 86b

The passage proceeds to point out further examples of the same parallels. The various actions of God in favor of Israel correspond to the concrete actions of Abraham for God or the angels. The comparison of Abraham's actions to those of God invites the notion that God is represented as incarnate. But in this instance we are not compelled to a reading of God as an essentially corporeal being. The actions God does can be accomplished in some less material or physical way. In the balance, however, we do find evidence to suggest that the authorship of the Bavli understood that God looks like a human being, specifically, like a man, and that God does what human beings of a particular order or class do.

3

God Incarnate in the Everyday World

In the final stage of the formation of the Judaism of the dual Torah, in the Talmud of Babylonia, God emerged as a fully exposed personality. The character of divinity encompassed God's virtue, the specific traits of character and personality that God exhibited above and here below. Above all, humility, the virtue sages most often asked of themselves, characterized the divinity. God wanted people to be humble, and God therefore showed humility.

> Said R. Joshua b. Levi, "When Moses came down from before the Holy One, blessed be he, Satan came and asked [God], 'Lord of the world, Where is the Torah?'
>
> "He said to him, 'I have given it to the earth....' [Satan ultimately was told by God to look for the Torah by finding the son of Amram.]
>
> "He went to Moses and asked him, 'Where is the Torah which the Holy One, blessed be he, gave you?'
>
> "He said to him, 'Who am I that the Holy One, blessed be he, should give me the Torah?'
>
> "Said the Holy One, blessed be he, to Moses, 'Moses, you are a liar!'
>
> "He said to him, 'Lord of the world, you have a treasure in store which you have enjoyed every day. Shall I keep it to myself?'
>
> "He said to him, 'Moses, since you have acted with hu-

mility, it will bear your name: "Remember the Torah of Moses, my servant" (Mal. 3:22).' "

b Shab. 89a

God here is represented as favoring humility and rewarding the humble with honor. What is important is that God does not here cite Scripture or merely paraphrase it; the conversation is an exchange between two vivid personalities. True enough, Moses, not God, is the hero. But the personality of God emerges in a vivid way. The following passage shows how traits imputed to God also define proper conduct for sages, not to mention other human beings.

At issue once again is humility, considered the imitation of God. Arrogance — the opposite — is treated as denial of God:

> And R. Yohanan said in the name of R. Simeon b. Yohai, "Whoever is arrogant is as if he worships idolatry.
>
> "Here it is written, 'Everyone who is arrogant in heart is an abomination to the Lord' (Prov. 16:5), and elsewhere it is written, 'You will not bring an abomination into your house' " (Deut. 7:26).
>
> And R. Yohanan on his own account said, "He is as if he denied the very Principle [of the world],
>
> "as it is said, 'Your heart will be lifted up and you will forget the Lord your God' " (Deut. 8:14).
>
> R. Hama bar Haninah said, "He is as if he had sexual relations with all of those women forbidden to him on the laws of incest.
>
> "Here it is written, 'Everyone who is arrogant in heart is an abomination to the Lord' (Prov. 16:5), and elsewhere it is written, 'For all these abominations ...' " (Lev. 18:27).
>
> Ulla said, "It is as if he built a high place,
>
> "as it is said, 'Cease you from man, whose breath is in his nostrils, for wherein is he to be accounted of' (Isa. 2:22).
>
> "Do not read, 'wherein,' but rather, 'high place.' "

b Sot. 5b, XVI

Whence [in Scripture] do we derive an admonition against the arrogant?

Raba said that Zeiri said, " 'Listen and give ear, do not be proud' " (Jer. 13:15).

R. Nahman bar Isaac said, "From the following: 'Your heart will be lifted up, and you will forget the Lord your God' (Deut. 8:14).

"And it is written, 'Beware, lest you forget the Lord your God' " (Deut. 8:11).

And that accords with what R. Abin said R. Ilaa said.

For R. Abin said R. Ilaa said, "In every place in which it is said, 'Beware lest . . . that you not, . . . ' the meaning is only to lay down a negative commandment [so that one who does such a thing violates a negative admonition]."

b Sot. 5b, XVIII

"With him also who is of a contrite and humble spirit" (Isa. 57:15).

R. Huna and R. Hisda:

One said, "I [God] am with the contrite."

The other said, "I [God] am the contrite."

Logic favors the view of him who has said, "I [God] am with the contrite," for lo, the Holy One, blessed be he, neglected all mountains and heights and brought his presence to rest on Mount Sinai,

and he did not raise Mount Sinai upward [to himself].

R. Joseph said, "A person should always learn from the attitude of his Creator, for lo, the Holy One, blessed be he, neglected all mountains and heights and brought his presence to rest on Mount Sinai,

"and he neglected all valuable trees and brought his presence to rest in the bush."

b Sot. 5b XX

Said R. Eleazar, "Whoever is arrogant is worthy of being cut down like an asherah [a tree that is worshiped].

"Here it is written, 'The high ones of stature shall be cut down' (Isa. 10:33),

"and elsewhere it is written, 'And you shall hew down their Asherim' " (Deut. 7:5).

And R. Eleazar said, "Whoever is arrogant — his dust will not be stirred up [in the resurrection of the dead].

"For it is said, 'Awake and sing, you that dwell in the dust' (Isa. 26:19).

"It is stated not 'you who lie in the dust' but 'you who dwell in the dust,' meaning, one who has become a neighbor to the dust [by constant humility] even in his lifetime."

And R. Eleazar said, "For whoever is arrogant the presence of God laments,

"as it is said, 'But the haughty he knows from afar' " (Ps. 138:6).

b Sot. 5b XXI

R. Avira expounded, and some say it was R. Eleazar, "Come and take note of the fact that not like the trait of the Holy One, blessed be he, is the trait of flesh and blood.

"The trait of flesh and blood is that those who are high take note of those who are high, but the one who is high does not take note of the one who is low.

"But the trait of the Holy One, blessed be he, is not that way. He is high, but he takes note of the low,

"as it is said, 'For though the Lord is high, yet he takes note of the low' " (Ps. 138:6).

b Sot. 5b XXII

Said R. Hisda, and some say it was Mar Uqba, "Concerning whoever is arrogant said the Holy One, blessed be he, he and I cannot live in the same world,

"as it is said, 'Whoever slanders his neighbor in secret — him will I destroy; him who has a haughty look and a proud heart I will not endure' (Ps. 101:5).

"Do not read, 'him [I cannot endure]' but 'with him [I cannot endure].' "

There are those who apply the foregoing teaching to those who slander, as it is said, "Whoever slanders his neighbor in secret — him will I destroy" (Ps. 101:5).

b Sot. 5b XXIII

Said R. Joshua b. Levi, "Come and take note of how great are the humble in the sight of the Holy One, blessed be he.

"For when the sanctuary stood, a person would bring a burnt-offering, gaining thereby the reward for bringing a burnt-offering, or a meal-offering, and gaining the reward for a meal offering.

"But a person who is genuinely humble does Scripture treat as if he had made offerings of all the sacrifices,

"as it is said, 'The sacrifices [plural] of God are a broken spirit' (Ps. 51:19).

"And not only so, but his prayer is not rejected, as it is said, 'A broken and contrite heart, O God, you will not despise' " (Ps. 51:19).

b Sot. 5b XXIX

The repertoire shows clearly that sages impute to God those traits of personality that are recommended and claim that God favors personalities like God's own. The clear implication is that God and the human being are consubstantial as to attitudes, emotions, and other aspects of virtue.

God laughs just as does a human being. The attribution to God of a sense of humor portrays the divinity once more as incarnate, the model by which the human being was made not only in physical form, but also in personality traits. God's laughter is not only because of delight. It may also take on a sardonic character, for instance, as ridicule:

Said R. Yose, "In the age to come idolators will come and convert [to Judaism]...and will put phylacteries on their foreheads and arms, place show-fringes on their garments and a *mezuzah* on their doorposts. When, however, the battle of Gog and Magog takes place, they will be asked, 'Why have you come?'

"They will reply, 'Against God and his anointed...' (Ps. 2:1).

"Then each of the converts will toss off the religious emblems and leave...and the Holy One, blessed be he, will sit and laugh,

"as it is said, 'He who sits in heaven laughs...' " (Ps. 2:4).

b A. Z. 3b

The repertoire of God's emotions encompasses not only desirable, but also undesirable traits. God not only exhibits and favors humility and has the capacity to laugh out of both joy and ridicule. God also becomes angry and performs acts that express that anger:

> And said R. Yohanan in the name of R. Yose, "How do we know that one should not placate a person when he is angry?
>
> "It is in line with the following verse of Scripture: 'My face will go and then I will give you rest' (Exod. 33:14).
>
> "Said the Holy One, blessed be he, to Moses, 'Wait until my angry countenance passes, and then I shall give you rest.' "
>
> But does the Holy One, blessed be he, get angry?
>
> Indeed so.
>
> For it has been taught on Tannaite authority:
>
> "A God that is angry every day" (Ps. 7:12).
>
> And how long is this anger going to last?
>
> A moment.
>
> And how long is a moment?
>
> It is one hundred fifty-eight thousand eight hundred and eighty-eighth part of an hour.
>
> And no creature except for the wicked Balaam has ever been able to fix the moment exactly.
>
> For concerning him it has been written, "He knows the knowledge of the Most High" (Num. 24:16).
>
> Now if Balaam did not even know what his beast was thinking, was he likely to know what the Most High is thinking?
>
> But this teaches that he knew exactly how to reckon the very moment that the Holy One, blessed be he, would be angry.
>
> That is in line with what the prophet said to Israel, "O my people, remember now what Balak, king of Moab, devised, and what Balaam, son of Beor, answered him ... that you may know the righteous acts of the Lord" (Mic. 6:5).
>
> Said R. Eleazar, "The Holy One, blessed be he, said to Is-

rael, 'Know that I did any number of acts of righteousness with you, for I did not get angry in the time of the wicked Balaam. For had I gotten angry, not one of (the enemies of) Israel would have survived, not a remnant.'

"That is in line with what Balaam said to Balak, 'How shall I curse whom God has not cursed, and how shall I execrate whom the Lord has not execrated?' (Num. 23:8).

"This teaches that for that entire time [God] did not get mad."

And how long is God's anger?

It is a moment.

And how long is a moment?

Said R. Abin and, some say, R. Abina, "A moment lasts as long as it takes to say 'a moment.' "

And how do we know that a moment is how long God is angry?

For it is said, "For his anger is but for a moment, his favor is for a lifetime" (Ps. 30:6).

If you like, you may derive the lesson from the following: "Hide yourself for a little while until the anger be past" (Isa. 26:20).

And when is God angry?

Said Abayye, "It is during the first three hours of the day, when the comb of the cock is white, and it stands on one foot."

But it stands on one foot every hour.

To be sure, it stands on its foot every hour, but in all the others it has red streaks, and in the moment at hand there are no red streaks [in the comb of the cock].

b Ber. 7A, LI

What is striking in this sizable account is the characterization of God's anger in entirely corporeal terms. God not only becomes angry; God also acts in anger. For one example, in anger God loses his temper:

Said R. Judah said Rab, "When the Holy One, blessed be he, proposed to create the world, he said to the angelic prince of the sea, 'Open your mouth and swallow all the water in the world.'

"He said to him, 'Lord of the world, it is quite sufficient if I stick with what I already have.'

"Forthwith he kicked him with his foot and killed him.

"For it is written, 'He stirs up the sea with his power, and by his understanding he smites through Rahab' " (Job 26:12).

b B.B. 74b

Like a human being, God thus can lose his temper. God's anger derives not only from ill temper but deeper causes. God is dissatisfied with the world as it is and so expresses anger with the present condition of humanity, on account of Israel:

For it has been taught on Tannaite authority:

R. Eliezer says, "The night is divided into three watches, and [in heaven] over each watch the Holy One, blessed be he, sits and roars like a lion,

"as it is said, 'The Lord roars from on high and raises his voice from his holy habitation, roaring he does roar because of his fold' (Jer. 25:30).

"The indication of each watch is as follows: at the first watch, an ass brays, at the second, dogs yelp, at the third, an infant sucks at its mother's breast or a woman whispers to her husband."

b Ber. 3A, VI

Said R. Isaac bar Samuel in the name of Rab, "The night is divided into three watches, and over each watch, the Holy One, blessed be he, sits and roars like a lion.

"He says, 'Woe to the children, on account of whose sins I have wiped out my house and burned my palace, and whom I have exiled among the nations of the world."

b Ber. 3A, VII

It has been taught on Tannaite authority:

Said R. Yose, "Once I was going along the way, and I went into one of the ruins of Jerusalem to pray. Elijah, of blessed memory, came and watched over me at the door until I had finished my prayer. After I had finished my prayer, he said to me, 'Peace be to you, my lord.'

"And I said to him, 'Peace be to you, my lord and teacher.'

"And he said to me, 'My son, on what account did you go into this ruin?'

"And I said to him, 'To pray.'

"And he said to me, 'You would have done better to pray on the road....'

"And he said to me, 'My son, what sound did you hear in this ruin?'

"I said to him, 'I heard the sound of an echo moaning like a pigeon and saying, "Woe to the children, on account of whose sins I have wiped out my house and burned my palace and whom I have exiled among the nations of the world.'"

"He said to me, 'By your life and the life of your head, it is not only at this moment that the echo speaks in such a way, but three times daily, it says the same thing.

" 'And not only so, but when Israelites go into synagogues and schoolhouses and respond, "May the great name be blessed," the Holy One shakes his head and says, "Happy is the king, whom they praise in his house in such a way! What does a father have, who has exiled his children? And woe to the children who are exiled from their father's table!" ' "

b Ber. 3A, VIII

God's anger and mourning form emotions identical to those of human beings, as is made explicit. Israel is God's children, and God mourns for them as a parent mourns for children who have suffered. The personality of God therefore takes the form of representing God's attitudes as the same as those of human beings, though of a cosmic order. But God's anger derives from broader causes than Israel's current condition.

The humanity of God emerges in yet another way. God enters into transactions with human beings and accords with the rules that govern those relationships. So God exhibits precisely the social attributes that human beings do. A number of stories, rather protracted and detailed, tell the story of God as a social being, living among and doing business with mortals. These stories provide extended portraits of God's relationships, in particular arguments with important figures, such as angelic figures, as well as Moses, David, and Hosea. In them God negotiates, persuades, teaches, argues, exchanges reasons. The personality of God therefore comes to expression in a variety of portraits of how God engages in arguments with men and angels, and so enters into the existence of ordinary people. These disputes, negotiations, and transactions yield a portrait of a God who is reasonable and capable of give and take, as in the following:

> Rabbah bar Mari said, "What is the meaning of this verse: 'But they were rebellious at the sea, even at the Red Sea; nonetheless he saved them for his name's sake' (Ps. 106:7)?
>
> "This teaches that the Israelites were rebellious at that time, saying, 'Just as we will go up on this side, so the Egyptians will go up on the other side.' Said the Holy One, blessed be he, to the angelic prince who reigns over the sea, 'Cast them [the Israelites] out on dry land.'
>
> "He said before him, 'Lord of the world, is there any case of a slave [namely, myself] to whom his master [you] gives a gift [the Israelites], and then the master goes and takes [the gift] away again? [You gave me the Israelites, now you want to take them away and place them on dry land.]'
>
> "He said to him, 'I'll give you one and a half times their number.'
>
> "He said before him, 'Lord of the world, is there a possibility that a slave can claim anything against his master? [How do I know that you will really do it?]'
>
> "He said to him, 'The Kishon brook will be my pledge [that I shall carry out my word. Nine hundred chariots at the brook were sunk (Jud. 3:23), while Pharaoh at the sea had only six hundred, thus a pledge one and a half times greater than the sum at issue.]'
>
> "Forthwith [the angelic prince of the sea] spit them out onto dry land, for it is written, 'And the Israelites saw the Egyptians dead on the sea shore' " (Exod. 14:30).
>
> B. Ar. 15A–B

God is willing to give a pledge to guarantee his word. He furthermore sees the right claim of the counterpart actor in the story. Hence we see how God obeys precisely the same social laws of exchange and reason that govern other incarnate beings. Still more interesting is the picture of God's argument with Abraham. God is represented as accepting accountability, by the standards of humanity, for what God does.

> Said R. Isaac, "When the Temple was destroyed, the Holy One, blessed be he, found Abraham standing in the Temple. He said to him, 'What is my beloved doing in my house?'
>
> "He said to him, 'I have come because of what is going on with my children.'
>
> "He said to him, 'Your children sinned and have been sent into exile.'
>
> "He said to him, 'But wasn't it by mistake that they sinned?'
>
> "He said to him, 'She has wrought lewdness' (Jer. 11:15).
>
> "He said to him, 'But wasn't it just a minority of them that did it?'
>
> "He said to him, 'It was a majority' (Jer. 11:15).
>
> "He said to him, 'You should at least have taken account of the covenant of circumcision [which should have secured forgiveness despite their sin]!'
>
> "He said to him, 'The holy flesh is passed from you' (Jer. 11:15).
>
> "And if you had waited for them, they might have repented!'
>
> "He said to him, 'When you do evil, then you are happy' (Jer. 11:15).
>
> "He said to him, 'He put his hands on his head, crying out and weeping, saying to them, 'God forbid! Perhaps they have no remedy at all!'
>
> "A heavenly voice came forth and said, 'The Lord called you "a leafy olive tree, fair with excellent fruit"' (Jer. 11:16).

" 'Just as in the case of an olive tree, its future comes only at the end [that is, it is only after a long while that it attains its best fruit], so in the case of Israel, their future comes at the end of their time.' "

b Men. 53b

God relates to Abraham as to an equal. That is shown by God's implicit agreement that he is answerable to Abraham for what has taken place with the destruction of the Temple. God does not impose on Abraham silence, saying that that is a decree not to be contested but only accepted. God as a social being accepts that he must provide sound reasons for his actions, as must any other reasonable person in a world governed by rules applicable to everyone. Abraham is a fine choice for the protagonist, since he engaged in the argument concerning Sodom. His complaint is expressed at B: God is now called to explain himself. At each point then Abraham offers arguments in behalf of sinning Israel, and God responds, item by item. The climax of course has God promising Israel a future worth having. God emerges as both just and merciful, reasonable but sympathetic. The transaction attests to God's conformity to rules of reasoned transactions in a coherent society.

The same picture is drawn in still greater detail when God engages Hosea in discussion. Here, however, Hosea complains against Israel, and God takes the part of Abraham in the earlier account. God's social role is defined in the model of the sage or master, a role we shall presently find prominent in the repertoire of portraits of personality. God teaches Hosea by providing an analogy for Hosea of what Hosea proposes that God do.

Said the Holy One, blessed be he, to Hosea, "Your children have sinned."

He should have said to him, "They are your children, children of those to whom you have shown grace, children of Abraham, Isaac, and Jacob. Send your mercy to them."

It is not enough that he did not say the right thing, but he said to him, "Lord of the world, the entire world is yours. Trade them in for some other nation."

Said the Holy One, blessed be he, "What shall I then do with that elder? I shall tell him, 'Go, marry a whore and have children of prostitution.' Then I'll tell him, 'Divorce her.' If he can send her away, then I'll send away Israel.'

For it is said, "And the Lord said to Hosea, Go, take a whore and have children of prostitution" (Hos. 1:1).

After he had two sons and a daughter, the Holy One, blessed be he, said to Hosea, "Should you not have learned the lesson of your master, Moses? Once I had entered into discourse with him, he separated from his wife. So you too, take your leave of her."

He said to him, "Lord of the world, I have children from her, and I simply cannot drive her out or divorce her."

Said to him the Holy One, blessed be he, "Now if you, married to a whore, with children of prostitution, and you don't even know whether they're yours or whether they come from some other fathers, are in such a state, as to Israel, who are my children, children of those whom I have tested, the children of Abraham, Isaac and Jacob. . . .

" . . . how can you say to me, 'Trade them in for some other nation'?"

When [Hosea] realized that he had sinned, he arose to seek mercy for himself. Said the Holy One, blessed be he, to him, "Instead of seeking mercy for yourself, seek mercy for Israel, against whom I have on your account issued three decrees [exile, rejection, and without compassion, reflecting the names of his children]."

He went and sought mercy and [God] annulled [the decrees] and gave them this blessing: "Yet the number of the children of Israel shall be as the sand of the sea . . . and instead of being called 'You are not my people,' they will be called 'You are the children of the living God.' And the children of Judah and the children of Israel shall be gathered together. . . . And I will show her to me in the land, and have compassion on her who was not treated with compassion and say to those who were not my people, 'You are my people' " (Hos. 2:1–2, 25).

B Pes 87a

Hosea negotiates with God, proposing that God reject Israel for some other nation. God's reply is that of an experienced teacher. He puts the disciple through a concrete lesson, which imparts to the disciple the desired experience and leads to the disciple's drawing the right conclusion. The social transaction then is worked out in accord with rules of reason. Just as experience teaches Hosea the lesson that one does not reject, but forgives, sinful relations, so Hosea draws the correct conclusion. The story then portrays God in a social transaction that is governed by accepted laws of orderly conduct.

God's relationships with David, a paramount theme in the story of David's sin with Bath Sheba, yield the picture of how God responds in a reasonable way to a reasonable proposal. Then, to be sure, God teaches a lesson of right conduct. But throughout God's role remains the same: a social and rational being, like mortals. What is important for my argument is the representation of God as engaged in negotiation in accord with rules that apply to heaven and earth alike. God then enters into society as a full participant in the world of humanity and plays a role that forms the counterpart to that of any just person. The personality of God here takes the now well established form of God as fully engaged in social transactions with counterparts on earth. We consider only those portions of the protracted story that pertain to our topic:

> Said R. Judah said Rab, "One should never put himself to the test, for lo, David, king of Israel, put himself to the test and he stumbled.
>
> "He said before him, 'Lord of the world, on what account do people say, "God of Abraham, God of Isaac, and God of Jacob," but they do not say, "God of David"?'
>
> "He said to him, 'They endured a test for me, while you have not endured a test for me.'
>
> "He said before him, 'Lord of the world, here I am. Test me.'
>
> "For it is said, 'Examine me, O Lord, and try me' (Ps. 26:1).
>
> "He said to him, 'I shall test you, and I shall do for you something that I did not do for them. I did not in-

form them [what I was doing], while I shall tell you what I
am going to do. I shall try you with a matter having to do
with sexual relations.'

"Forthwith: 'And it came to pass in an eventide that
David arose from off his bed'" (2 Sam. 11:2).

The opening passage represents God in conversation with
David and responsive to David's reasoning. This is more than
the presence of God familiar in the earliest strata of the canon,
and God in conversation with David forms a personality, not
the mere "you" of prayer familiar in the initial writings of the
Judaism of the dual Torah. Where God cites Scripture, it is not
merely to prove a point but to make a statement particular to
the exchange at hand. So it is not a conventional portrait of
God's serving as the voice of an established text. It is, to the
contrary, the picture of God engaged in a social transaction
with a sentient being.

We skip the description of David's relationship with Bath
Sheba and move directly to David's plea of forgiveness. In the
passages that follow, God serves merely as audience for David's
statements:

> Raba interpreted Scripture, asking, "What is the mean-
> ing of the following verse: 'To the chief musician, a Psalm
> of David. In the Lord I put my trust, how do you say to my
> soul, Flee as a bird to your mountain?' (Ps. 11:1)?
>
> "Said David before the Holy One, blessed be he, 'Lord
> of the world, Forgive me for that sin, so that people should
> not say, "The mountain that is among you [that is, your
> king] has been driven off by a bird." ' "
>
> Raba interpreted Scripture, asking, "What is the mean-
> ing of the following verse: 'Against you, you alone, have
> I sinned, and done this evil in your sight, that you might
> be justified when you speak and be clear when you judge'
> (Ps. 11:1)?
>
> "Said David before the Holy One, blessed be he, 'Lord of
> the world. It is perfectly clear to you that if I had wanted
> to overcome my impulse to do evil, I should have done
> so. But I had in mind that people not say, "The slave has

conquered the Master [God, and should then be included as 'God of David']." ' "

Raba interpreted Scripture, asking, "What is the meaning of the following verse: 'For I am ready to halt and my sorrow is continually before me' (Ps. 38:18)?

"Bath Sheba, daughter of Eliam, was designated for David from the six days of creation, but she came to him through anguish."

And so did a Tannaite authority of the house of R. Ishmael [teach], "Bath Sheba, daughter of Eliam, was designated for David, but he 'ate' her while she was yet unripe."

Raba interpreted Scripture, asking, "What is the meaning of the following verse: 'But in my adversity they rejoiced and gathered themselves together, yes, the abjects gathered themselves together against me and I did not know it, they tore me and did not cease' (Ps. 35:15)?

"Said David before the Holy One, blessed be he, 'Lord of the world, it is perfectly clear to you that if they had torn my flesh, my blood would not have flowed [because I was so embarrassed].

" 'Not only so, but when they take up the four modes of execution inflicted by a court, they interrupt their Mishnah study and say to me, "David, he who has sexual relations with a married woman — how is he put to death?"

" 'I say to them, "He who has sexual relations with a married woman is put to death through strangulation, but he has a share in the world to come," while he who humiliates his fellow in public has no share in the world to come.' "

Now God emerges once more and plays the role of antagonist to David's protagonist:

R. Dosetai of Biri interpreted Scripture, "To what may David be likened? To a gentile merchant.

"Said David before the Holy One, blessed be he, 'Lord of the world, "Who can understand his errors?" ' (Ps. 19:13).

"He said to him, 'They are remitted for you.'

" 'Cleanse me of hidden faults' (Ps. 19:13).

" 'They are remitted to you.'

" ' "Keep back your servant also from presumptuous sins" ' (Ps. 19:13).

" 'They are remitted to you.'

" ' "Let them not have dominion over me, then I shall be upright" (Ps. 19:13), so that the rabbis will not hold me up as an example.'

" 'They are remitted to you.'

" ' "And I shall be innocent of great transgression" (Ps. 19:13), so that they will not write down my ruin.'

"He said to him, 'That is not possible. Now if the Y that I took away from the name of Sarah [changing it from Sarai to Sarah] stood crying for so many years until Joshua came and I added the Y [removed from Sarah's name] to his name, as it is said, "And Moses called Oshea, the son of Nun, Jehoshua" (Num. 13:16), how much the more will a complete passage of Scripture [cry out if I remove that passage from its rightful place]!' "

God once more emerges as a fully formed personality. For God's role here is not merely to cite Scripture. God can do just so much, but no more, and this detail is the contribution not of Scripture but of the storyteller. The personality of God once more takes shape in the notion of God as bound by rules of procedure and conduct. God enters into civil and rational transactions with human beings and conforms to the same rules. with the result that is expressed here.

"And I shall be innocent from great transgression" (Ps. 19:13):

He said before him, "Lord of the world, forgive me for the whole of that sin [as though I had never done it]."

He said to him, "Solomon, your son, even now is destined to say in his wisdom, 'Can a man take fire in his bosom, and his clothes not be burned? Can one go upon hot coals, and his feet not be burned? So he who goes in to his neighbor's wife, whoever touches her shall not be innocent' " (Prov. 6:27–29).

He said to him, "Will I be so deeply troubled?"

He said to him, "Accept suffering [as atonement]."
He accepted the suffering.

Said R. Judah said Rab, "For six months David was afflicted with saraat, and the presence of God left him, and the sanhedrin abandoned him.

"He was afflicted with saraat, as it is written, 'Purge me with hyssop and I shall be clean, wash me and I shall be whiter than snow' (Ps. 51:9).

"The presence of God left him, as it is written, 'Restore to me the joy of your salvation and uphold me with your free spirit' (Ps. 51:14).

"The sanhedrin abandoned him, as it is written, 'Let those who fear you turn to me and those who have known your testimonies' (Ps. 119:79).

"How do we know that this lasted for six months? As it is written, 'And the days that David rules over Israel were forty years: [107B] Seven years he reigned in Hebron, and thirty-three years he reigned in Jerusalem' (1 Kgs. 2:11).

"Elsewhere it is written, 'In Hebron he reigned over Judah seven years and six months' (2 Sam. 5:5).

"So the six months were not taken into account. Accordingly, he was afflicted with saraat [for such a one is regarded as a corpse].

"He said before him, 'Lord of the world, forgive me for that sin.'

" 'It is forgiven to you.'

" ' "Then show me a token for good, that they who hate me may see it and be ashamed, because you, Lord, have helped me and comforted me" (Ps. 86:17).'

"He said to him, 'While you are alive, I shall not reveal [the fact that you are forgiven], but I shall reveal it in the lifetime of your son, Solomon.'

"When Solomon had built the house of the sanctuary, he tried to bring the ark into the house of the Holy of Holies. The gates cleaved to one another. He recited twenty-four prayers [Freedman, *The Babylonian Talmud*, 734, n. 4: in 2 Chr. 6 words for prayer, supplication, and hymn occur twenty-four times], but was not answered.

"He said, 'Lift up your head, O you gates, and be lifted up, you everlasting doors, and the King of glory shall come in. Who is this King of glory? The Lord strong and might, the Lord mighty in battle' (Ps. 24:7ff.).

"And it is further said, 'Lift up your heads, O you gates even lift them up, you everlasting doors' (Ps. 24:7).

"But he was not answered.

"When he said, 'Lord God, turn not away the face of your anointed, remember the mercies of David, your servant' (2 Chr. 6:42), forthwith he was answered.

"At that moment the faces of David's enemies turned as black as the bottom of a pot, for all Israel knew that the Holy One, blessed be he, had forgiven him for that sin."

b San. 106b–107a, CCXLVI–CCLI

As we see, our hero is not God but David. The story is not told to characterize God, who plays a supporting part, if not that of a mere straight man. Nonetheless, the portrayal of God justifies the claim that we have here an incarnate God, consubstantial with humanity not only in physical and emotional traits, but also, and especially, in the conformity to the social laws of correct transactions that, in theory at least, make society possible.

Among the available models for the personality of God — warrior, teacher, young man — the one that predominated entailed representation of God as sage. God is represented as a schoolmaster:

"He sits and teaches school children, as it is said, 'Whom shall one teach knowledge, and whom shall one make to understand the message? Those who are weaned from milk' " (Isa. 28:9).

b A. Z. 3b

But this is not the same as God as a master sage teaching mature disciples, that is, God as rabbi and sage. That representation emerges in a variety of ways and proves the single most important mode of the personality of God. God's personality merged throughout with the Bavli authorship's representation of the personality of the ideal master or sage. That representation in the Bavli proved detailed and specific. A sage's life — Torah learned, then taught, through discipleship — encompassed both the correct modes of discourse and ritual argument, on the one side, and the recasting of all relationships in accord with received convention of courtesy and subservience. God then is represented in both dimensions, as a master requiring correct conduct of his disciples and as a teacher able to hold his own in arguments conducted in accord with the prevailing ritual. For one example, a master had the right to demand an appropriate greeting, and God, not receiving that greeting, asked why:

> Said R. Joshua b. Levi, "When Moses came up on high, he found the Holy One, blessed be he, tying crowns onto the letters of the Torah. He said to him, 'Moses, don't people say hello in your town?'
>
> "He said to him, 'Does a servant greet his master [first]?'
>
> "He said to him, 'You should have helped me [at least by greeting me and wishing me success].'
>
> "He said to him, 'Now I pray you let the power of the Lord be great, just as you have said' " (Num. 14:17).

Moses here plays the role of disciple to God the teacher, a persistent pattern throughout. Not having offered the appropriate greeting, the hapless disciple is instructed on the matter. Part of the ritual of "being a sage" thus comes to expression. Yet another detail of that same ritual taught how to make a request — and how not to do so. A request offered in humility is proper; one made in an arrogant or demanding spirit is not. Knowing what to ask is as important as knowing how. The congregation of Israel shows how not to do so, and God shows, nonetheless, the right mode of response, in the following:

> The congregation of Israel made its request in an improper way, but the Holy One, blessed be he, responded in a proper way.
>
> For it is said, [the congregation of Israel said to God,] "And let us know, eagerly strive to know, the Lord, the

Lord's going forth is sure as the morning, and the Lord shall come to us as the rain" (Hos. 6:3).

Said the Holy One, blessed be he, to [the congregation of Israel,] "My daughter, now you are asking for something which sometimes is wanted and sometimes is not really wanted. But I shall give you something which is always wanted.

"For it is said, 'I will be as dew to Israel' " (Hos. 14:6).

Further, [the congregation of Israel] made its request in an improper manner, "O God, set me as a seal on your heart, as a seal on your arm" (Song 8:6).

[But the Holy One, blessed be he, responded in a proper way.] Said the Holy One, blessed be he, to [the congregation of Israel,] "My daughter, now you are asking for something which sometimes can be seen and sometimes cannot be seen. But I shall give you something which can always be seen.

"For it is said, 'Behold, I have graven you on the palms of my hands' (Isa. 49:16) [and the palms are always visible, in a way in which the heart and arm are not]."

b Ta. 4a

Dew is always wanted, rain not. To be a seal on the heart or arm is to be displayed only occasionally. But the hands are always visible. Consequently, God as sage teaches Israel as disciple how to make a proper request.

The status of sage, expressed in rituals of proper conduct, is attained through knowing how to participate in argument about matters of the Torah, particularly the law. Indeed, what makes a sage an authority is knowledge of details of the law. Consequently, my claim that God is represented as a particular sort of human being, namely, as a sage, requires evidence that God not only follows the arguments (as above, "My sons have conquered me!") and even has opinions which he proposes to interject, but also himself participates in debates on the law. Ability to follow those debates and forcefully to contribute to them forms the chief indicator. That that ability joins some men to God is furthermore explicit. So the arguments in the academy in heaven, over which God presides, form the exact counterpart to the arguments on earth, with the result that God emerges as precisely consubstantial, physically and intellectually, with the particular configuration of the sage:

> In the session in the firmament, people were debating this question: if the bright spot came before the white hair, the person is unclean. If the white hair came before the bright spot, he is clean. What about a case of doubt?
>
> The Holy One, blessed be he, said, "Clean."
>
> And the rest of the fellowship of the firmament said, "Unclean."
>
> They said, "Who will settle the matter?"
>
> It should be Rabbah b. Nahmani, for he is the one who said, "I am an expert in the laws of plagues and in the effects of contamination through the overshadowing of a corpse...."
>
> A letter fell down from the sky to Pumbedita: "Rabbah b. Nahmani has been called up by the academy of the firmament...."
>
> b B. M. 86a

God in this story forms part of the background of action. Part of a much longer account attached to the academy of Pumbedita of how Rabbah b. Nahmani was taken up to heaven, the story shows us how God is represented in a heavenly session of the heavenly academy studying precisely those details of the Torah — here Leviticus 13 as restated in Mishnah tractate Negaim — as were mastered by the great sages of the day. That the rest of the heavenly court would disagree forms an essential detail, because it verifies the picture and validates the claim, to come, that heaven required the knowledge of the heroic sage. That is the point of B–C–D. Then Rabbah b. Nahmani is called to heaven — that is, killed and transported upward — to make the required ruling. God is not the centerpiece of the story. The detail that a letter was sent from the heavenly academy to the one on earth, at Pumbedita, then restates the basic point of the story, the correspondence of earth to heaven on just this matter.

In the image of the sage, however, God towers over other sages, disposes of their lives, and determines their destinies. Portraying God as sage allowed the storytellers to state in a vivid way convictions on the disparity between sages' great intellectual achievements and their this-worldly standing and fate. But God remains within the model of other sages, takes up the rulings, follows the arguments, participates in the sessions that distinguish sages and mark them off from all other people:

> Said R. Judah said Rab, "When Moses went up to the height, he found the Holy One, blessed be he, sitting and tying crowns to the letters [of the Torah]."
>
> "He said to him, 'Lord of the universe, why is this necessary?'
>
> "He said to him, 'There is a certain man who is going to come into being at the end of some generations, by the name of Aqiba b. Joseph. He is going to find expositions to attach mounds and mounds of laws to each point [of a crown].'
>
> "He said to him, 'Lord of the universe, show him to me.'
>
> "He said to him, 'Turn around.'
>
> "[Moses] went and took his seat at the end of eight rows, but he could not understand what the people were saying. He felt weak. When discourse came to a certain matter, one of [Aqiba's] disciples said to him, 'My lord, how do you know this?'
>
> "He said to him, 'It is a law revealed by God to Moses at Mount Sinai.'
>
> "Moses' spirits were restored.
>
> "He turned back and returned to the Holy One, blessed be he. He said to him, 'Lord of the universe, now if you have such a man available, how can you give the Torah through me?'
>
> "He said to him, 'Be silent. That is how I have decided matters.'
>
> "He said to him, 'Lord of the universe, you have now shown me his mastery of the Torah. Now show me his reward.'
>
> "He said to him, 'Turn around.'
>
> "He turned around and saw people weighing out his flesh in the butcher-shop.

"He said to him, 'Lord of the universe, such is his
mastery of Torah, and such is his reward?'

"He said to him, 'Be silent. That is how I have decided
matters.'"

b Men. 29b

This is the single most important narrative in the Bavli's repertoire of allusions to, and stories about, the personality of God.
For God's role in the story is hero and principal actor. He is no
longer the mere interlocutor, nor does he simply answer questions of the principal voice by citing Scripture. Quite to the
contrary, God makes all the decisions and guides the unfolding
of the story. Moses then appears as the straight man. He asks
the questions that permit God to make the stunning replies.
Why do you need crowns on the letters of the Torah? Aqiba will
explain them, by tying laws to these trivial and opaque details.
What are these laws? I cannot follow them. Aqiba will nonetheless attribute them to you. Why then give the Torah through
me instead of him, since he understands it and I do not? It is
my decree. Finally, comes the climax: what will this man's reward be? His flesh will be weighed out in butcher shops. The
response remains the same. Moses, who is called "our rabbi"
and forms the prototype and ideal of the sage, does not understand. God then tells him to shut up and accept his decree.
God does what he likes, with whom he likes. Perhaps the storyteller had in mind a polemic against rebellious brilliance and
for dumb subservience. But that does not seem to me the urgent
message, which rather requires acceptance of God's decrees,
whatever they are, when the undeserving receive glory, when
the accomplished come to nothing. That God emerges as a fully
formed personality — the model for the sage — hardly requires
restatement.

Just as Israel glorifies God, so God responds and celebrates
Israel. In the passages at hand the complete personality of God,
in physical, emotional, and social traits, comes to expression.
God wears phylacteries, an indication of a corporeal sort. God
further forms the correct attitude toward Israel, which is one of
love, an indication of an attitude on the part of divinity corre-
sponding to right attitudes on the part of human beings. Finally,

to close the circle, just as there is a "you" to whom humanity prays, so God too says prayers — to God, and the point of these prayers is that God should elicit from himself forgiveness for Israel:

> Said R. Nahman bar Isaac to R. Hiyya bar Abin, "As to the phylacteries of the Lord of the world, what is written in them?"
>
> He said to him, " 'And who is like your people Israel, a singular nation on earth' " (1 Chr. 17:21).
>
> "And does the Holy One, blessed be he, sing praises for Israel?"
>
> "Yes, for it is written, 'You have avouched the Lord this day ... and the Lord has avouched you this day' (Deut. 26:17, 18).
>
> "Said the Holy One, blessed be he, to Israel, 'You have made me a singular entity in the world, and I shall make you a singular entity in the world.
>
> " 'You have made me a singular entity in the world,' as it is said, 'Hear O Israel, the Lord, our God, the Lord is one' (Deut. 6:4).
>
> " 'And I shall make you a singular entity in the world,' as it is said, 'And who is like your people, Israel, a singular nation in the earth' " (1 Chr. 17:21).
>
> Said R. Aha, son of Raba to R. Ashi, "That takes care of one of the four subdivisions of the phylactery. What is written in the others?"
>
> He said to him, " 'For what great nation is there.... And what great nation is there...' (Deut. 4:7, 8), 'Happy are you, O Israel...' (Deut. 33:29), 'Or has God tried,...' (Deut. 4:34). And 'To make you high above all nations'" (Deut. 26:19).
>
> "If so, there are too many boxes!"
>
> "But the verses, 'For what great nation is there' and 'And what great nation is there,' which are equivalent, are in one box, and 'Happy are you, O Israel' and 'Who is like your people Israel' are in one box, and 'Or has God tried,...' in one box, and 'To make you high' in one box.

"And all of them are written in the phylactery that is on the arm."

b Ber. 6A–B, XXXIX

Said R. Yoḥanan in the name of R. Yose, "How do we know that the Holy One, blessed be he, says prayers?

"Since it is said, 'Even them will I bring to my holy mountain and make them joyful in my house of prayer' (Isa. 56:7).

" 'Their house of prayer' is not stated, but rather, 'my house of prayer.'

"On the basis of that usage we see that the Holy One, blessed be he, says prayers."

What prayers does he say?

Said R. Zutra bar Tobiah said Rab, " 'May it be my will that my mercy overcome my anger, and that my mercy prevail over my attributes, so that I may treat my children in accord with the trait of mercy and in their regard go beyond the strict measure of the law.' "

b Ber. 7A, XLIX

It has been taught on Tannaite authority:

Said R. Ishmael b. Elisha, "One time I went in to offer up incense on the innermost altar, and I saw the crown of the Lord, enthroned on the highest throne, and he said to me, 'Ishmael, my son, bless me.'

"I said to him, 'May it be your will that your mercy overcome your anger, and that your mercy prevail over your attributes, so that you treat your children in accord with the trait of mercy and in their regard go beyond the strict measure of the law.'

"And he nodded his head to me."

And from that story we learn that the blessing of a common person should not be negligible in your view.

b Ber. 7A, L.

The corporeal side to the personality of God is clear at the outset: God wears phylacteries. The consubstantial traits of attitude and feeling — just as humanity feels joy, so does God; just as humanity celebrates God, so does God celebrate Israel — are made explicit. The social transactions of personality are specified as well. Just as Israel declares God to be unique, so God declares Israel to be unique. And just as Israel prays to God, so God says prayers. What God asks of God is that God transcend God — which is what, in prayer, humanity asks for as well. In the end, therefore, to be "in our image, after our likeness," the power of the powerless, the riches of the disinherited, the valuation and valorization of the will of those who have no right to will is not to be the mirror-image of God but very much to be like God.

Part Two

God in Christ: Christ in God

BRUCE CHILTON

4

Jesus' Claim to the Divine World

Narrative Identity:
Creating Self by Telling Tales

The Jesus we meet in a great deal of discussion recently, especially in "the Jesus Seminar," would be at home in a lecture hall or an academic seminar, but you might be surprised to find him in a synagogue. But that is just where Luke places him at the start of his public activity, in a scene which is consonant with the Gospels as a whole. Jesus comes to Nazareth, where he was brought up, and goes to synagogue on the Sabbath, as was his habit. He is given a scroll containing the book of Isaiah, in accordance with the regular practice of that congregation (Luke 4:15–17).

So far everything that happens is predictable and routine. It only needs emphasizing because some scholars have encouraged us to forget or to marginalize Jesus' Judaism. But then there is an odd turn in the events in the synagogue, and the oddity concerns Jesus' retelling of Scripture. For his reading is no simple reading, but a transforming of the book of Isaiah. He says,

> The spirit of the Lord is upon me,
>   because he has anointed me
> to announce news of triumph to the poor.
> He has sent me to preach release to prisoners,
>   and renewal of sight to the blind,
> to send the oppressed into release,
> to preach the acceptable year of the Lord.

Once Jesus has said this, people stare at him, and finally they reject what he says. What is the surprise; what is the offense? First, Jesus' "reading" is no reading. He here drops a phrase from the relevant chapter of Isaiah (61:1–2), and adds one of his own, a phrase that speaks of giving renewal of sight to the blind. Reference to the blind in Aramaic of the period of Jesus often refers to those who do not see the meaning of the Torah,[1] and that is the sense of the expression here. Jesus is saying that, in retelling Scripture, he is making the meaning of Scripture clear to those who were blind. The reason for surprise and growing opposition in the synagogue becomes more apparent, especially when Jesus goes on to say, "Today this Scripture is fulfilled in your ears" (Luke 4:21). He claims to speak in the ears of the congregation in the interests of opening their eyes.

Whether Jesus cited Scripture or told parables of his own invention, his purpose was the same. He framed a particular argument, characteristic of his message and of Christianity ever since. He claimed that God's power could be perceived as a kingdom, and that the kingdom of God was the basis on which our lives could be transformed. You could see it in the book of Isaiah or in mustard seed, but whether in a text or in a field the point of the kingdom of God was that it needed to be acknowledged and joined in order to be entered.

The field in which a seed grows changes with the growth. A text in which the kingdom is experienced is also transformed. Isaiah is different as a result of being retold in the interests of the kingdom: the text could be changed, and was changed, and Jesus insisted on changing it. Not just here, but time and again, he cites the book of Isaiah and other texts in forms which are not attested in Hebrew or Greek or Aramaic. To some extent, that is because he was a popular rabbi, perhaps even illiterate, but that is only part of the reason. The more profound cause was that, in the vision of Jesus, the kingdom changed the way

---

1. In the Isaiah Targum, see 42:7, "to open the eyes of *the house of Israel who are as* blind *to the law* . . .". Italics represent innovations as compared to the Hebrew Bible, as in Bruce Chilton, *The Isaiah Targum: Introduction, Translation, Apparatus and Notes*, Aramaic Bible 11 (Edinburgh: T. & T. Clark; Wilmington: Glazier, 1987).

you saw the text, just as it changed the way you saw nature and people.[2]

In fact, it may well be that the Old Syriac version of Luke 4 provides an even more accurate impression of what Jesus said. Syriac is closely related to Aramaic, and there is evidence that oral traditions concerning Jesus may be reflected in the Old Syriac version. It has Jesus "cite" Isaiah in the following way:[3]

> The spirit of the Lord is upon *you,*
> because he has anointed *you*
> to announce news of triumph to the poor.
> He has sent me to preach release to prisoners,
> and renewal of sight to the blind,
> *and I will free the broken with* release,
> to preach the acceptable year of the Lord.

"To you the mystery of the kingdom of God has been given; but to those outside, everything happens in parables" (Mark 4:11). Retelling in the light of the kingdom seems to fracture texts and to turn the world around us into riddles, until we become part of the story that is told. Just as Jesus says, You do not put a light under a bushel, so he says, You are the light of the world (Matt. 5:14–16).

So here is a retelling which involves the awareness that you are part of the story which is told. The kingdom within the story reaches within you, and a new text, a fresh narrative, is the result. That is why, when Jesus tells his parables and cites Scripture, the question naturally comes, as it does in Nazareth, Who is this person (Luke 4:22–30)? Retelling a story so that it becomes a new story, he lays claim to a different self. He reshapes Scripture in the light of experience.[4]

---

2. For a fuller discussion, see Bruce Chilton, *A Galilean Rabbi and His Bible: Jesus' Use of the Interpreted Scripture of His Time,* Good News Studies 3 (Wilmington: Glazier, 1984; also published in the same year by SPCK in London with the subtitle *Jesus' Own Interpretation of Isaiah*).

3. Here, italics indicate deviations from the text already quoted. For a full discussion, see Bruce Chilton, *God in Strength: Jesus' Announcement of the Kingdom,* Studien zum Neuen Testament und seiner Umwelt 1 (Freistadt: Plöchl, 1979), 157–77. The monograph is also available in "The Biblical Seminar" (Sheffield: JSOT, 1987).

4. See also Jacob Neusner and Bruce Chilton, *Revelation: The Torah and the*

This is why christology is an inescapable issue in the study of the New Testament and of Christianity. Changing Scripture in the light of experience involves claiming the authority to do so; in the terms of reference of early Judaism, a messianic status is necessary to rearrange the elements of Scripture in the way Jesus does. Just as modern scholarship of Jesus has missed the point by marginalizing Jesus from his own Judaism, it has also missed the point by claiming that Jesus claimed no messianic status. It is perfectly true that he was suitably cautious about the *language* he used (above all, see Matt. 16:13–20; Mark 8:27–30; Luke 9:18–21). After all, he was one humble member of a subject people whose political aspirations were of concern to Rome. But there can be no doubt about his *implicit* claim to the messianic authority to explain what Scripture did not: how God was gathering his own people into his kingdom.

Jesus' self, then, his messianic identity, developed out of and was implicit in his retelling of Scripture. Accepting his account of the kingdom, devoting oneself to the power of the kingdom in transforming one's life, involved recognizing Jesus in his messianic role. That, in turn, also implied that the communities which formed around this recognition of the kingdom and of Jesus themselves retold Scripture, and in that retelling also apprehended a fresh identity. And that was precisely what happened.

A particular retelling, Paul's retelling of Abraham, will concern us in a moment. But in order to see that narrative, that formation of identity, in its originality, it is necessary to see the variety of retellings which were possible within primitive Christianity. The most familiar retelling among followers of Jesus in Jerusalem was associated with the community which centered on James, the brother of Jesus.[5] Here, the Davidic identity of Jesus was stressed, an identity which was consonant with James' own claims to preeminence in a group which de-

---

Bible, Christianity and Judaism — The Formative Categories 1 (Valley Forge, Pa.: Trinity Press International, 1995), 129–48.

5. For a fuller discussion of biblical interpretation within the circle of James, see Neusner and Chilton, *Revelation,* 118–23. The present example extends the textual base of passages which can be attributed to that circle.

fined itself by loyalty to the Temple as well as devotion to Jesus' teaching.

That group identified Jesus' Last Supper in precise terms with Passover; his final meal was a Seder, with all its attendant preparations (Matt. 26:17–20/Mark 14:12–17/Luke 22:7–14). So the group around James retold the Seder and retold the Last Supper at one and the same time.

Recent scholarship has rightly seen that the identification of the Last Supper with Passover is theologically motivated. After all, the Gospels themselves have the authorities resolve to deal with Jesus before the crowds of Passover arrived (Matt. 26:1–5/Mark 14:1–2/Luke 22:1–2). And the basic elements of the Seder — lamb, unleavened bread, bitter herbs (see Exod. 12:8) — are notable in the Last Supper itself only for their absence. By identifying Jesus' meal and Passover, however, the circle of James managed to limit full participation in Eucharist to those who were Jews, since circumcision was a strict requirement for males who took part in a Seder (according to Exod. 12:48–49). Non-Jews might meet at meals which convened according to the teaching of Jesus, but only Israelites could celebrate the covenantal meaning of the Last Supper. The circle of James carefully identifies its members with the specifically Davidic messiahship of Jesus.

Another approach is represented by a more famous community, the circle of Peter, discussed in volume 1 of our trilogy.[6] The Transfiguration at first (Matt. 17:1–8; Mark 9:2–8; Luke 9:28–36) evokes Jesus alongside Moses and Elijah (which is how Peter, James, and John see Jesus on the mountain, transformed before them). That vision is an implicit but powerful claim of Jesus' authority, owing to the place of Moses and Elijah within the biblical and postbiblical tradition. In his *Jewish Antiquities,* Josephus (writing around the year 94 C.E.) describes Moses, not as dying as in Deuteronomy 34:5, but as "disappearing" (so *Antiquities* 4 §326), which puts Moses in the same category with Elijah and Enoch, who did not die, but were taken up into

---

6. For discussion of the biblical interpretation characteristic of this group (in relation to the Transfiguration), see Neusner and Chilton, *Revelation,* 123–26.

heaven (so *Antiquities* 9 § 28). Moses and Elijah, Josephus shows us, were not simply venerated figures within early Judaism, but were understood to be the living and continuing sources of the Torah and of prophecy.

Jesus on the mountain of the Transfiguration, then, is associated with Moses on the mountain of the covenant (see Exod. 24) and with Elijah on the mountain of prophecy (see 1 Kings 19). Both those figures are associated with the Spirit of God within the biblical tradition. Moses is so filled with Spirit, he can
· bestow it on others (see Num. 11), and Elijah explains to his disciple Elisha how to attain double his own Spirit by witnessing his ascension (see 2 Kings 2). Just that emphasis was characteristic of the circle of Peter[7] and sustains the understanding within the Transfiguration of how Jesus may be compared to the primal agents of Torah and prophecy.

"This is my beloved son, hear him." That statement by the divine voice, as a cloud covers the scene, addresses the second major point of the Transfiguration. When the apostles are able to see again, only Jesus is there. Jesus' particular identity as one who bestows Spirit is therefore not expressed so as to invalidate Moses' agency of the Torah or Elijah's agency of prophecy. Sonship is what enables Jesus, risen from the dead, to receive the Holy Spirit from the Father and to pour it out on believers: that is what Peter argues at the scene of Pentecost in Acts 2 (see especially v. 33). The Transfiguration is a visionary narrative which anticipates the full power of Jesus' agency after his resurrection.

What relates Jesus to Moses and Elijah, and at the same time allows for the distinctive identities of each, is the Spirit of God and the possibility of its bestowal on others. Moses' particular agency of Spirit involves the giving of the Torah and its interpretation; Elijah's particular agency of Spirit involves the ever-strengthening witness of prophecy;[8] Jesus' particular

---

7. As is explained in Jacob Neusner and Bruce Chilton, *The Body of Faith: Israel and the Church,* Christianity and Judaism — the Formative Categories 2 (Valley Forge, Pa.: Trinity Press International, 1996), 129–33.

8. The well-known motif within early Judaism that prophecy was no longer available as it once had been did not imply any weakness of the prophetic principle as such. On the contrary, the hope was that the return of prophecy would herald the relegation of other forms of authority. So, for example, Simon is confirmed as high priest and leader only until "a faithful

agency of Spirit involves, not a new medium of its availability (such as Torah or prophecy), but direct access to the Spirit of God on the part of believers, communally and individually. But what the circle of Peter asserts, in setting Jesus alongside Moses and Elijah, begs the question of what to do if the Spirit as bestowed by Jesus appears to be in conflict with the witness of the Torah and of prophecy.

That was a particularly difficult question in the early Church, where there was a conflict between those who held that the Torah was upheld by Jesus, and those who held that Jesus transcended the Torah. Indeed, the conflict followed out of Jesus' own position. Those around James insisted that the Torah, with its rules of purity, must be observed by Jews; those around Peter permitted those rules to be relaxed to permit fellowship with non-Jews. Galatians 2 permits us to see how severe the tension of that conflict could become.[9]

Paul argues in Galatians that rules of purity are permanently suspended in Christ. He says that when believers hear with faith, they are "just as Abraham, who believed in God, and it was reckoned to him as righteousness" (Gal. 3:6). Paul understands the role of Abraham as being the patriarch of Judaism, but he argues that Abraham's faith, not his obedience to the law, made him righteous in the sight of God (Gal. 3:7):

> Know, therefore, that those who are of faith are sons of Abraham.

Believing in Jesus Christ as the Son of God — a belief crystallized in baptism within Paul's thought and the experience of primitive Christianity — opens the floodgates of God's Spirit. When the believer in baptism arises from the water and calls God "Father," he does so with the same Aramaic word Jesus

---

prophet should arise" (1 Macc. 14:41), and a decision about how properly to deal with the stones of the altar which had been desecrated is delayed until a prophet should adjudicate the matter (1 Macc. 4:46). That prophet was widely associated with Elijah (see Mal. 3:1–4:6).

9. For a discussion of that conflict, see Neusner and Chilton, *Revelation*, 112–23.

used (*Abba,* see Gal. 4:4–6). That is because the Spirit of God's own Son is sent by God into believers' hearts (4:6).

These three circles of primitive Christianity — Jacobean, Petrine, and Pauline — give us three different Christian identities. James re-presents the Seder at the Last Supper, with the result that the social self of the Church focuses on the restoration of Davidic hopes. Peter re-visions Sinai in the Transfiguration, so that Moses and Jesus together may guide their followers, who share an identity of vocation. Paul re-defines the setting and substance of Abraham's belief, and consequently removes genealogy from any reckoning of what makes the people of God.

The operative contention throughout is that something within the text, concerning Abraham or the exodus or Sinai, transcends the text. The quality of Abraham's faith is more important than what he believed in (namely, that he would have a son by Sarah); the liberation of the exodus is not only from Egypt, but is experienced when a new ground of authority is known in Eucharist; Sinai is revisited whenever, in Jesus' company, we come to know Moses and Elijah again.

All three styles of Christian interpretation, i.e., Paul's and James's and Peter's, are lineal descendants of Jesus'. His use of Scripture involved the use of selected passages together with the claim, "Today is this Scripture fulfilled in your hearing" (see Luke 4:16–21). Fulfillment involved the claim that specific aspects of Scripture were realized, while others were ignored, and that realization became the measure for the basic meaning of that passage and others. That is just where Jesus' method is analytic, where the Rabbinic method is comprehensive.[10] But that difference of method, which has been traced more fully in volume 1 of Christianity and Judaism — the Formative Categories series, is not simply a matter of interpretative technique. Rather, the distinctive approach to Scripture which characterized Jesus and his followers was a function of their conception and experience of God's activity in them and in the world.

---

10. See Chilton, *A Galilean Rabbi and His Bible.*

Fulfillment and the Dynamic of God

The changes which Jesus feels free to invoke, within sacred texts and within human experience, derived from his conviction that God was altering the world, and altering it irrevocably. The language Jesus used was that of God's kingdom, and by referring to it he shaped a particular view of God's activity. The parable of the mustard seed, to which we have already alluded, illustrates how dynamic Jesus conceived God's activity to be (Mark 4:30–32, compare Matt. 13:31–32; Luke 13:18–19):

> And he was saying, How shall we compare the kingdom of God, or in what parable shall we put it? As a seed of mustard, which when it is sown upon the earth is smaller than all the seeds which are upon the earth. But when it is sown, it arises and becomes greater than all the herbs and makes big branches, so that the birds of the heaven are able to dwell under its shadow.

That final, arresting image probably refers to the tree as symbolic of God's ultimate, all-embracing victory (see, for example, Ezek. 17:22–24). That picture, as well as the temporal terms of reference of the parable — emphatically between sowing and harvest — clearly shows that Jesus conceived of the kingdom as being eschatological. It was the definitive action of God, whose purpose was to change the world permanently.

Scholars have rightly seen that Jesus' preaching of the kingdom was not simply eschatological: it was not as if he was speaking of the future and not of the present. But in their effort to emphasize that Jesus' conception was more than eschatological, some of us have suggested it was less than eschatological.[11] That would amount to a falsification of Jesus' theology, because he was concerned passionately — as his parables richly attest — with how actual change in time represents the definitive power of God at the end of time. If the kingdom of God is read merely as a symbol, or a possibility of seeing things, the transforming power which Jesus claimed as of its very nature is overlooked.

---

11. So, for example, Marcus J. Borg, *Jesus in Contemporary Scholarship* (Valley Forge, Pa.: Trinity Press International, 1994).

But the recent challenge of eschatology as an adequate category for an understanding of Jesus is right in insisting that there is more to his conception of the kingdom. The mustard seed is not only effective at the end of time; its growth is proof that God is also active within our world, immanent, in the language of theology. Here, indeed, we come to one of the most characteristic aspects of Jesus' view of the kingdom. Its finality, and God's transcendence, were not taken to mean that the present was bereft of God. Rather, Jesus insisted that the world around us could be perceived with the hopefulness which comes of considering the mustard seed, as attesting the transformation which comes from God. God is transcendent, outside us, and yet he transforms us and our world from the inside out. Alongside the eschatological dimension of the kingdom, the dimension which looks to transformation over time, there is also a transcendent dimension, the dimension which sees space as occupied by the growing immanence of God.

Jesus' ability to speak of God's finality (in eschatological terms) and of God's immanence (in terms of his transcendence) is primarily what makes him difficult to understand. How can the same teacher who taught his followers to pray, "your kingdom come" (so Matt. 6:10; Luke 11:2) also claim that his own ministry showed that "the kingdom of God has come upon you" (so Matt. 12:28; Luke 11:20)? The answer is that the request for the kingdom is along the lines of the time in which one hopes for God to act, while the statement of the kingdom's coming is along the lines of the space which God has already — in his sovereign immanence — transformed.

Within theological discussion, a classic question has been posed by the relationship between the transcendence and the immanence of God. Divine transcendence may appear absolute, in that God cannot be reduced to what he created, but rather must be altogether unconditioned by what he has made. On the other hand, if God is to be known at all, there must be some sense in which he is immanent, present within his creation. Jesus' teaching of the kingdom of God resolves the puzzle of divine transcendence and immanence by means of a vision of God's activity within the world, an activity which is both final in terms of time and presently effective in terms of space.

Jesus did not limit his conception of God's activity to time and space alone. There are other dimensions of the kingdom to be considered. But those additional dimensions can seem confusing, until it is remembered that they are all functions of Jesus' basic insight that transcendence and immanence are not mutually exclusive qualities. Rather, they express means by which God may be envisioned and understood.

In addition to being final in terms of time and present in terms of space, Jesus conceived of God as perfect within the realm of ethics. The parable of the mustard seed imagines harvest as the goal of growth, and harvest is a time for gathering in what accords with God's will. That sense of the harvest is well established within the teaching of Jesus (for example, see Mark 4:26–29, just before the parable of the mustard seed). That is a reason for which readiness is such an important emphasis within Jesus' teaching.

Connected with the dimension of ethics, purity needs also to be considered. Although ethics and purity are evidently related, they are also distinct. Ethics refers to the goal of God's action, while purity refers to its conditions. Although the coming of the harvest as described in the parable is dramatic, its precedent is to be found in the quality of the tiny seed. For all that it is small, the offer of its growth is possible because of what it is and because of the soil in which it is sown. (Again, the relationship of the parable of the seed growing by itself, Mark 4:26–29, to the parable of the mustard seed, Mark 4:30–32, makes that point all the plainer.) Another dimension of Jesus' conception of the kingdom, then, regards the conditions which it demands for growth.

And finally, the kingdom is conceived along a last, fifth dimension in Jesus' conception; the parable of the mustard seed illustrates that dimension, as well. The birds which come to reside in the branches of the mustard are not only symbols of God's victory. They are that, as we have already suggested. But in addition, the image of the birds expresses a dimension of inclusion as being an essential aspect of the kingdom (see Ps. 104:10–17). The birds appear from afar, and are offered a dwelling without condition: the kingdom is established as that which reaches far to offer its power and protection.

These dimensions of the kingdom — its finality, immanence, perfection, purity, and inclusiveness — may be illustrated by means of many other sayings of Jesus.[12] The parable of the mustard seed is simply one example among many of how these five aspects, sometimes with one or more emphasized more than the others, relate to each other within Jesus' conception of God's activity.

Prayer: The Practice of Fulfillment

When Jesus' teaching of the kingdom of God is analyzed according to the dimensions of divine activity implicit within his conception, it can seem to be an abstract affair. Generations of scholars and readers and hearers of the parables have typically found them elusive and difficult to explain. But it would be a profound mistake to conceive of Jesus' teaching as setting up an intellectual puzzle, a paradox for its own sake. The point of the parables was rather to awaken the hearer to the possibility of a certain vision of God, a vision which might then be practiced by those who would follow Jesus.

Jesus' prayer is emblematic of this practical purpose within his ministry.[13] Although the kingdom of God formally constitutes one element with the Lord's Prayer, the dimensions of the kingdom are just the dimensions in which God is approached within the prayer (see Matt. 6:9–13; Luke 11:2–4). After God is invoked as "Father," the first act of the prayer is to sanctify God's name, to acclaim that it will be holy. That asserts purity as the basis on which God will act, and it also establishes that God himself, by disclosing his name and his character, will provide the foundation of all that he does. After God is approached as Father and the sanctification of his name is welcomed, the coming of his kingdom is also acclaimed. Purity and eschatology are put side by side as dimensions of God's disclosure of himself.

12. See Neusner and Chilton, *Revelation*, 131–40, and — for the most complete treatment — Bruce Chilton, *Pure Kingdom: Jesus' Vision of God*, Studying the Historical Jesus 1 (Grand Rapids: Eerdmans; London: SPCK, 1996).

13. For a more detailed development, see Bruce Chilton, *Jesus' Prayer and Jesus' Eucharist: His Personal Practice of Spirituality* (Valley Forge, Pa.: Trinity Press International, 1997).

The petitions which follow[14] relate immediately to the three other dimensions. Daily bread is asked for, and that is taken as a sign of God's inclusive provision. It is of interest that, in Ps. 104, birds making their nests and all creatures finding their sustenance are images of God's continuing and all-embracing care (see Psalm 104:10–30). In the Lord's Prayer, as well, what is asked for is that provision which God endows us with out of his limitless care for what he has made.

The forgiveness of sin has a particular place within the Lord's Prayer, in its assumption that the request is heeded by God. Forgiveness is required regularly, which is why it is included in Jesus' model for standard prayer, and yet the assumption is that it is also granted. That is, God's forgiveness is a regular, almost routine, example of his immanence: he reaches into our human relations in order to release us from the consequences of our own actions when we repent of them.

Finally, the Lord's Prayer closes with the request not to be led into temptation. Implicit in that petition is the awareness that judgment, God's own ethical standard, is something from which we might well defect. The Prayer therefore concludes with a vivid plea that we should never prove to be disloyal, never forget or disavow the One who is truly our Father.

As it turns out, then, the Lord's Prayer marks out a consciousness of God which is fully consistent with Jesus' preaching of the kingdom. In fact, both his preaching and his practice of prayer were geared to apprehend God's own activity and to join God in that activity, the disclosure of his kingdom. Formally, therefore, the solution of how God is in the world is that, within Christianity, the divine kingdom is precisely the dynamic by which God is present within, final for, and in the process of transforming the world.

Jesus' Teaching of Regeneration

Once God is understood, as kingdom, to be remaking his own creation, the entire issue of how God is in the world is put

---

14. And only these are petitions, directed to God in the second person. What precedes is in the third-person imperative, and the statements amount to acclamations.

in a new light. Instead of imagining the world as static and God as entering it, the picture is rather of the world as changing: people are changed within that world and are offered the prospect of entry into God's kingdom. Indeed, entry into the kingdom is one of the characteristic emphases within Jesus' teaching.

The comparison of the kingdom of God to invitations to a feast receives development in a full, narrative parable (Matt. 22:1–10; Luke 14:16–24; *Thomas* saying 64). Jesus tells a story of people's misguided attention to matters which are ordinarily seen as important. Consumed by the business of the day (in Matthew, even to the point of violence), they spurn the offer of a banquet which will not come around again. The motifs of the parable are also developed within Rabbinic literature.

A similar parable is attributed to Yoḥanan ben Zakkai (a younger contemporary of Jesus') in which a king invited his servants to a feast, without announcing the precise time of the meal.[15] Wise servants attired themselves properly and waited at the door of the king's house. Foolish servants expected definite signs of the meal's preparation beforehand and went about their work until they should see them. When the king appeared without further ado, the wise enjoyed a fine meal; the foolish servants in their work-soiled clothing were allowed to enter, but were made to stand and watch while the others ate.

The essential emphasis, shared in Jesus' parable and Yoḥanan ben Zakkai's, is on the overriding nature of the king's command: ordinary duties are superseded by the royal invitation. Indeed, once the king invites, attention to what is usually thought of as commendable activity is punished; nothing is to distract one from the feast which is one's goal. In its implicit conception of the kingdom, the parable (from "Q," once again in quite different versions in Matthew and Luke) presents no substantial difference from the parable attributed to Yoḥanan. In each, routine dutifulness is presented as an inhibition to entry into the kingdom. Moreover, the kingdom is viewed, from the

---

15. In the Babylonian Talmud, see Shabbath 153a; see Chilton, *Pure Kingdom*, 74–76.

point of view of judgment, as that into which one might or might not enter.

Entry into the kingdom is possible because it is already available, as a transcendence which may already be perceived (the second coordinate). Because the kingdom is currently within one's field of vision, devotion to mere duty — to anything which excludes the kingdom — can only slight the king. Once available, the kingdom can only either be entered or rejected.

The fundamental similarity between Jesus' parable and Yoḥanan's permits us to see by comparison those elements which are especially heightened within Jesus'. First, a wider range of activities is named, which causes those invited to miss the appointed time of the invitation. Yoḥanan speaks only of people getting soiled working in the king's field; Jesus pictures people with farms and businesses (and extravagant weddings, in Luke and *Thomas*) of their own. The activities specified presuppose disposable wealth, so that a warning against riches is inherent in the parable (see also Matt. 19:23–24; Mark 10:23–25; Luke 18:24–25, and Jesus' saying concerning God and the Aramaic term "mammon," Matt. 6:24; Luke 16:13). Although the wealth which enables distraction is criticized in the parable, Jesus here primarily calls attention to the consequence of the distractions themselves.

In all three versions of Jesus' parable (each of which is distinctive), an unusual resistance to the king's invitation is also at issue. As Joachim Jeremias notes, sending servants out to escort guests to a feast was a special act of courtesy; the assumption of the parable is that those invited have long known of the feast.[16] Their obstinacy in refusing to attend a banquet they have long known of is another characteristic emphasis in Jesus' parable, along with his warning against the kind of distraction which wealth brings. Of course, their obstinacy and their distraction are related to one another. Activities which cause the invitation to be spurned (not merely declined) are by definition willful rejections of the feast, disastrous, self-imposed inhibitions from entering a household greater than one's own can ever be.

---

16. See Joachim Jeremias, *The Parables of Jesus*, trans. S. H. Hooke (London: SCM, 1972), 176.

Against those inhibitions, Jesus' host offers a new invitation, to those whose low status virtually assures their willingness to come. That willingness is all that commends them. They have not been more enthusiastic, more obedient, or more patient than those originally invited: their response is their only virtue. Where attentiveness is what Yohanan's parable insists upon (at the cost of duty), Jesus' parable insists that rough alacrity will triumph over the business of the day.

That which is available, the feast whose invitations have already been issued, can either be accepted or rejected. The fact, in Jesus' understanding, that the transcendent kingdom is already immanent, that the king's servants have been sent to collect guests for the feast, means that judgment is already being worked out in terms of who agrees to be gathered in and who resists on the excuse of wealthy business.

We have looked at this parable in some detail because it makes unmistakably clear how emphatic Jesus was that the kingdom of God demanded radical change in order to be entered. Conventional notions of duty and loyalty were inadequate and needed to be superseded by a completely new ethic for the kingdom.

Together with a new ethic, Jesus also pictured life with God as involving a regeneration of who we are, such that ordinary human relationships would no longer prevail. Some Sadducees are portrayed as asking a mocking question of Jesus, designed to disprove the possibility of resurrection. Because Moses commanded that, were a man to die childless, his brother should raise up a seed for him, suppose there were seven brothers, the first of whom was married. If they all died childless in sequence, whose wife would the woman be in the resurrection? (see Matt. 22:23–28; Mark 12:18–23; Luke 20:27–33).

Jesus' response is categorical and direct (following Mark 12:24–27, compare Matt. 22:29–32; Luke 20:34–38):

You completely deceive yourselves, knowing neither the Scriptures nor the power of God! Because when they arise from the dead, they neither marry nor are given in marriage, but are as angels in the heavens. But concerning the dead, that they rise, have you not read in the book of Moses about the bush, when God spoke to him, I am the God of Abraham and the God of Isaac and the God or Jacob? He is not God of the dead but of the living. You deceive yourselves greatly.

The second argument, the argument from Scripture, is the more straightforward, an appeal both to the nature of God and to the evaluation of the patriarchs in early Judaism. If God identifies himself with Abraham, Isaac, and Jacob, it must be that in his sight they live. And those three patriarchs are indeed living principles of Judaism itself; they are Israel as chosen in the case of Abraham (see Gen. 15), as redeemed in the case of Isaac (see Gen. 22), and as struggling to identity in the case of Jacob (see Gen. 32). But that implicit logic of that second argument only makes the first argument seem all the bolder by comparison.

The direct comparison between people in the resurrection and angels is fully consonant with the thought that the patriarchs must live in the sight of God, since angels are normally associated with God's throne (so, for example, Dan. 7:9–14). But Jesus' statement is not only a theoretical assertion of the majesty of God; it is also an emphatic claim of what we might call divine anthropology. He asserts that human relations, the usual basis of human society and divisions among people (namely, sexual identity), are radically altered in the resurrection.[17] That claim of substantial regeneration became a major theme among the more theological thinkers who followed Jesus.

---

17. It is commonly asserted that Jesus accorded with accepted understandings of resurrection within Judaism; see Pheme Perkins, *Resurrection: New Testament Witness and Contemporary Reflection* (London: Chapman, 1984), 75. That is an unobjectionable finding, but it leads to an odd conclusion: "Nor can one presume that Jesus makes any significant contribution to or elaboration of these common modes of speaking." Perkins is not clear about what she means here, or the basis of her assertion. Does warning the reader against presuming that Jesus had something original to say imply that he in fact said nothing original? Why speak of presumption at all, when there is an actual saying to hand? But the analysis of the saying is also confused, because Perkins speaks of it as invented by Mark when it has anything new to say, and as routine insofar as it may be attributed to Jesus. The discussion typifies the ill-defined program of trivializing the place of Jesus within the tradition of the New Testament by critics who once tended to exaggerate the literary aspirations of those who composed the documents.

The Metaphysics of the Resurrection in Paul

Paul's discussion of the issue of the resurrection in 1 Corinthians 15 clearly represents his continuing commitment to the categorical understanding of the resurrection which Jesus initiated. The particular occasion of his teaching is the denial of the resurrection on the part of some people in Corinth (1 Cor. 15:12b): "how can some of you say that there is not a resurrection of the dead?" His address of that denial is first of all on the basis of the integrity of apostolic preaching. Indeed, Paul precedes his question with the earliest extant record of the traditions regarding Jesus' resurrection (1 Cor. 15:1–11). That enables Paul to press on to his first argument against the Corinthian denial of the resurrection (15:13–14): "But if there is no resurrection of the dead, neither has Christ been raised; and if Christ has not been raised, then our preaching is empty and your faith is empty!"

Paul expands on this argument in what follows (1 Cor. 15:15–19), but the gist of what he says in that section is as simple as what he says at first: faith in Jesus' resurrection requires our affirmation of the reality of resurrection generally. That may seem to be an argument entirely from hypothesis, until we remember that Paul sees the moment when belief in Jesus occurs as the occasion of our reception of the Spirit of God (so Gal. 4:4–6):

> When the fullness of time came, God sent forth his Son, born from woman, born under law, so that he might redeem those under law, in order that we might obtain Sonship. And because you are sons, God sent the Spirit of his Son into your hearts, crying, "Abba! Father!"

Because the Spirit in baptism is nothing other than the living Spirit of God's Son, Jesus' resurrection is attested by the very fact of the primordial Christian experience of faith. The availability of his Spirit shows that he has been raised from the dead. In addition, the preaching in his name formally claims his resurrection, so that to deny resurrection as a whole is to make the apostolic preaching into a lie: empty preaching, as Paul says, and therefore empty faith.

Paul's emphasis on the spiritual integrity of the apostolic

preaching, attested in baptismal experience, is coherent with Jesus' earlier claim that the Scriptures warrant the resurrection (since God is God of the living, rather than of the dead). Implicitly, apostolic preaching is accorded the same sort of authority which Jesus attributed to the Scriptures of Israel. Paul also proceeds — in a manner comparable to Jesus' argument (but in the reverse order) — to an argument on the basis of the category of humanity which the resurrection involves: he proceeds to portray Jesus as the first of those raised from the dead. His resurrection is what provides hope for the resurrection of the dead as a whole (1 Cor. 15:20–28).

That hope, Paul goes on to argue, is what permits the Corinthians themselves to engage in the practice of being baptized on behalf of the dead (15:29).[18] The practice assumes that, when the dead come to be raised, even if they have not been baptized during life, baptism on their behalf after their death will confer benefit. Similarly, Paul takes his own courage as an example of the hopeful attitude which must assume the resurrection of the dead as its ground: why else would Christians encounter the dangers that they do (15:30–32a)?

The claim of resurrection, then, does not only involve a hope based upon a reception of Spirit and the hopeful promise of Scripture (whether in the form of the Scriptures of Israel or the apostolic preaching). Resurrection as an actual hope impinges directly upon what we conceive becomes of persons as we presently know them after they have died. (And that, of course, will immediately influence our conception of people as they now are and how we might engage with them.) Paul's argument therefore cannot and does not rest solely on assertions of the spiritual integrity of the biblical witness and the apostolic preaching. He must also spell out an anthropology of resurrection, such that the spiritual hope and the scriptural witness are worked out within the terms of reference of human experience.

Precisely when he does that in 1 Corinthians 15, Paul develops a Christian metaphysics. He does so by comparing people in the resurrection, not to angels, as Jesus himself had done,

---

18. For a discussion of the practice in relation to Judaic custom, see Ethelbert Stauffer, *New Testament Theology*, trans. J. Marsh (New York: Macmillan, 1955), 299 n. 544.

but to the resurrected Jesus. And that comparison functions for
Paul both (as we have already seen) because Jesus is preached
as raised from the dead and because, within the experience
of baptism, Jesus is known as the living source of the Spirit
of God.[19] Jesus as raised from the dead is the point of departure for Paul's thinking about the resurrection, and because his
focus is a human being, his analysis of the resurrection is much
more systematic than Jesus'. When Paul thinks of a person, he
conceives of a body as composed of flesh, physical substance
which varies from one created thing to another (for example,
people, animals, birds, and fish (1 Cor. 15:35–39). But in addition to being physical bodies, people are also what Paul calls a
"psychic body," that is, bodies with souls (1 Cor. 15:44). (Un-
fortunately, the phrase is wrongly translated in many modern
versions, but its dependence on the noun for "soul" [*psukhe*] is
obvious. The adjective does not mean "physical" as we use that
word.) In other words, people as bodies are not just lumps of
flesh, but they are self-aware. That self-awareness is precisely
what makes them a "psychic body."

Now in addition to being physical body and psychic body,
Paul says we are (or can be, within the power of resurrection)
"spiritual body" (1 Cor. 15:44): "it is sown a psychic body, it
is raised a spiritual body." That is, we can relate thoughts and
feelings to one another and to God. The explanation of how
spirit may be the medium of God's communication is developed
earlier in 1 Corinthians (2:10–11). Paul develops his position by
quoting a passage from Isaiah 64:4 (in 2:9), which speaks of
things beyond human understanding which God has readied
for those who love him, and Paul then goes on to say (2:10–11):

> God has revealed them to us through the Spirit; for the
> Spirit searches all things, even the depths of God. For who
> knows a person's affairs except the person's spirit within?
> So also no one has known God's affairs except the Spirit
> of God.

---

19. As Perkins (227) puts it, "These associations make it clear that the resurrection of Jesus had been understood from an early time as the eschatological
turning point of the ages and not merely as the reward for Jesus as a righteous
individual."

Here a simple question masks a profound thought. As Paul sees human relations, one person can know what another thinks and feels only on the basis of their shared "spirit." "Spirit" is the name for what links one person with another, and by means of that link we can also know what God thinks and feels. The spirit at issue, Paul goes on to say, is not "the spirit of the world," but "the Spirit of God" (1 Cor. 2:12): the medium of ordinary, human exchange becomes in baptism the vehicle of divine revelation.

Paul's remark in 1 Corinthians 2 is part of a complete anthropology, which is spelled out further in 1 Corinthians 15. Jesus on the basis of the resurrection is the last Adam, a life-giving spirit (1 Cor. 15:45) just as the first Adam was a living being or soul (the two words are the same in Greek, *psukhe*). Jesus is the basis on which we can realize our identities as God's children, the brothers and sisters of Christ, and know the power of the resurrection. In so saying, Paul defines a distinctive christology as well as a characteristic spirituality. The metaphysics of both, which relate Christ to creation and believers to God, is predicated upon a regeneration of human nature. "Flesh" and "soul" become, not ends in themselves, but way stations on the way to "Spirit."

Origen and the Refinement of Spiritual Resurrection

Born in 185 in Egypt, Origen knew the consequences which faith could have in the Roman world: his father died in the persecution of Severus in 202. Origen accepted the sort of renunciation demanded of apostles in the Gospels, putting aside his possessions to develop what Eusebius calls the philosophical life demanded by Jesus (see Eusebius, *History of the Church* 6.3). His learning resulted in his appointment to the catechetical school in Alexandria, following the great examples of Pantaenus and Clement. Origen later moved to Caesarea in Palestine, as a result of a bitter dispute with Demetrius, the bishop of Alexandria. Indeed, Origen remained a controversial figure after his death (and until this day), to a large extent because he wrestled more profoundly than most thinkers with the consequences of Spirit's claim on the flesh.

The dispute surrounding Origen specifically included his sexuality. According to Eusebius, as part of his acceptance of evangelical precepts of renunciation, Origen took literally the reference in Matthew to people making eunuchs of themselves for the sake of the kingdom of heaven (Matt. 19:12). Accordingly, he emasculated himself (*History of the Church* 6.8). As Eusebius immediately goes on to say, Demetrius later capitalized on the story, by using it to discredit Origen. Scholarship has been divided over the question of whether Origen in fact castrated himself.

The scholarly debate about Origen's genitals is less interesting than the fact that there has been such a debate. If Origen did castrate himself, the argument has been (since the time of Eusebius!), it must have been because his interpretation of Scripture was literal at that stage of his life. If he did not, Demetrius must have invented the story. Castration is the extreme and negative form of the celibacy encouraged and required within Christian circles from the second century onward; the physical cutting crosses the line between renunciation and mutilation. Whether the act is taken to have been performed on Origen's body or only in Demetrius's mind, no one defends it. The story about Origen violates the axiom (articulated by Paul in 1 Cor. 6:19) that the human body, as an actual or potential vehicle of the divine, is not to be desecrated.

In fact, Origen himself argued against any literal interpretation of Matthew 19:12, insisting that it did not refer to self-mutilation.[20] The passage has been used to suggest that Origen did castrate himself and later saw the error of the act, as well as to argue that he never would have done such a thing. The matter is not likely ever to be settled, but what Origen did settle to his own satisfaction was the fraught issue of the relationship between flesh and spirit, the tension between which produced the plausibility of the claim that a great Christian teacher might castrate himself. But where the reputation of Origen has been stalled in the antithesis between flesh and spirit,

---

20. See Jean Daniélou, *Origen,* trans. W. Mitchell (New York: Sheed and Ward, 1955), 13.

his own thought was productive precisely because he worked out a dialectical reconciliation between the two.

In his treatment of the resurrection, Origen shows himself a brilliant exegete and a profound theologian. He sees clearly that, in 1 Corinthians 15, Paul insists that the resurrection from the dead must be bodily. And Origen provides the logical grounding of Paul's claim (*On First Principles* 2.10.1):

> If it is certain that we are to be possessed of bodies, and if those bodies that have fallen are declared to rise again — and the expression "rise again" could not properly be used except of that which had previously fallen — then there can be no doubt that these bodies rise again in order that at the resurrection we may once more be clothed with them.

But Origen equally insists upon Paul's assertion that "flesh and blood cannot inherit the kingdom of God" (1 Cor. 15:50). There must be a radical transition from flesh to spirit, as God fashions a body which can dwell in the heavens (*On First Principles* 2.10.3).

Origen pursues the point of this transition into a debate with fellow Christians (*On First Principles* 2.10.3):

> We now direct the discussion to some of our own people, who either from want of intellect or from lack of instruction introduce an exceedingly low and mean idea of the resurrection of the body. We ask these men in what manner they think that the "psychic body" will, by the grace of the resurrection, be changed and become "spiritual"; and in what manner they think that what is sown "in dishonor" is to "rise in glory," and what is sown "in corruption" is to be transformed into "incorruption." Certainly if they believe the Apostle, who says that the body, when it rises in glory and in power and in incorruptibility, has already become spiritual, it seems absurd and contrary to the meaning of the Apostle to say that it is still entangled in the passions of flesh and blood.

Origen's emphatic denial of a physical understanding of the resurrection is especially interesting for two reasons.

First, his confidence in the assertion attests the strength of his conviction that such an understanding is "low and mean": the problem is not that physical resurrection is unbelievable, but that the conception is unworthy of the hope that faith speaks of. Origen's argument presupposes, of course, that a physical understanding of the resurrection was current in Christian Alexandria. But he insists, again following Paul's analysis, that the body which is raised in resurrection is continuous with the physical body in principle, but different from it in substance (*On First Principles* 2.10.3):

> So our bodies should be supposed to fall like a grain of wheat into the earth, but implanted in them is the cause that maintains the essence of the body. Although the bodies die and are corrupted and scattered, nevertheless by the word of God that same cause that has all along been safe in the essence of the body raises them up from the earth and restores and refashions them, just as the power that exists in a grain of wheat refashions and restores the grain, after its corruption and death, into a body with stalk and ear. And so in the case of those who shall be counted worthy of obtaining an inheritance in the kingdom of heaven, the cause before mentioned, by which the body is refashioned, at the order of God refashions out of the earthly and animate body a spiritual body, which can dwell in heaven.

The direction and orientation of Origen's analysis is defined by his concern to describe what in humanity may be regarded as ultimately compatible with the divine. For that reason, physical survival is rejected as an adequate category for explaining the resurrection. Instead, he emphasizes the change of substance that must be involved.

Second, the force behind Origen's assertion is categorical. The resolution of the stated contradictions — namely, "psychic"/"spiritual," "dishonor"/"glory," and "corruption"/ "incorruption" — involves taking Paul's language as directly applicable to the human condition. In the case of each contradiction, the first item in the pair needs to yield to the spiritual progression of the second item in the pair. That is the progressive logic of Origen's thought, now applied comprehensively to human experience.

In Origen's articulation, progressive thinking insists upon the radical transition which resurrection involves. Although his discussion is a brilliant exegesis of Paul's argument, Origen also elevates the progressive principle above any other consideration which Paul introduces. What had been in Paul a method for understanding Scripture which was applicable outside that field becomes in Origen the fundamental principle of global spiritual revolution. Only that, in his mind, can do justice to the promise of being raised from the dead.

For all that the transition from flesh to spirit is radical, Origen is also clear that personal continuity is involved. To put the matter positively, one is clothed bodily with one's own body, as we have already seen. To put the matter negatively, sins borne by the body of flesh may be thought of as visited upon the body which is raised from the dead (*On First Principles* 2.10.8):

> Just as the saints will receive back the very bodies in which they have lived in holiness and purity during their stay in the habitations of this life, but bright and glorious as a result of the resurrection, so, too, the impious, who in this life have loved the darkness of error and the night of ignorance will after the resurrection be clothed with murky and black bodies, in order that this very gloom of ignorance, which in the present world has taken possession of the inner parts of their mind, may in the world to come be revealed through the garment of their outward body.

Although Origen is quite consciously engaging in speculation at this point, he firmly rejects the notion that the flesh is involved in the resurrection, even when biblical promises appear to envisage earthly joys (*On First Principles* 2.11.2):

> Now some men, who reject the labor of thinking and seek after the outward and literal meaning of the law, or rather give way to their own desires and lusts, disciples of the mere letter, consider that the promises of the future are to be looked for in the form of pleasure and bodily luxury.

And chiefly on this account they desire after the resurrection to have flesh of such a sort that they will never lack the power to eat and drink and to do all things that pertain to flesh and blood, not following the teaching of the apostle Paul about the resurrection of a "spiritual body."

His reasons for rejecting such a millenarian view are both exegetical and theological. Paul is the ground of the apostolic authority he invokes, in a reading we have already seen. He uses that perspective to consider the Scriptures generally (*On First Principles* 2.11.3). But Origen deepens his argument from interpretation with a deeply theological argument. He maintains that the most urgent longing is the desire "to learn the design of those things which we perceive to have been made by God." This longing is as basic to our minds as the eye is to the body: constitutionally, we long for the vision of God (*On First Principles* 2.11.4).

The manner in which Origen develops his own thought is complex, involving a notion of education in paradise prior to one's entry into the realm of heaven proper (*On First Principles* 2.11.6):

I think that the saints when they depart from this life will remain in some place situated on the earth, which the divine Scripture calls "paradise." This will be a place of learning and, so to speak, a lecture room or school for souls, in which they may be taught about all that they had seen on earth and may also receive some indication of what is to follow in the future. Just as when placed in this life they had obtained certain indications of the future, seen indeed "through a glass darkly," and yet truly seen "in part," they are revealed more openly and clearly to the saints in the proper places and times. If anyone is of truly pure heart and of clean mind and well-trained understanding he will make swifter progress and quickly ascend to the region of the air, until he reaches the kingdom of heaven, passing through the series of those "mansions," if I may so call them, which the Greeks have termed spheres — that is, globes — but which the divine Scripture calls heavens.

Even this brief excerpt from a convoluted description represents the complexity of Origen's vision, but two factors remain plain and simple. First, the vision of God is the moving element through the entire discussion. Second, Origen clearly represents and develops a construction of the Christian faith in which eschatology has been swallowed up in an emphasis upon transcendence. The only time which truly matters is that time until one's personal death, which determines one's experience in paradise and in the resurrection. "Heaven" as a cosmographic place now occupies the central position once occupied by the eschatological kingdom of God in Jesus' teaching. That, too, occurs on the authority of progressive dialectics, the refinement of Pauline metaphysics.

Augustine and the History of Resurrection

Augustine (354–430) was bishop of Hippo in North Africa. Born in North Africa of humble origins, Augustine had prospered as a professor of rhetoric until his conversion to Christianity while he was in Milan. From there he made his way back to North Africa and was leading a life of philosophical leisure until he was called to Hippo for ordination to the priesthood, and eventually service as bishop. There, in addition to a full pastoral ministry, Augustine wrote some of the most influential works in the development of Western culture. His *Confessions* is an examination of his own life and his own heart in the interests of exploring the human soul, and his treatise *On the Trinity* is a classic of philosophical theology and spirituality. *On the City of God* is a monumental achievement, a reflection on the history of the world in light of the will of God.

Within that truly global history, discussion of eschatology is a necessary part of the work, and Augustine frames classic and orthodox responses to some of the most persistent questions of the Christian theology of his time. He adheres to the expectation of the resurrection of the flesh, not simply of the body (as had been the manner of Origen). In so doing, he refutes the Manichaean philosophy which he accepted prior to his conversion to Christianity. In Manichaeanism, named after a Persian teacher of the third century named Mani, light and darkness are two eternal substances which struggle against one another, and they war over the creation they have both participated in making.[21] As in the case of Gnosticism, on which it was dependent, Manichaeanism counseled a denial of the flesh. By his insistence on the resurrection of the flesh, Augustine revives the strong assertion of the extent of God's embrace of his own creation (in the tradition of Irenaeus, the great millenarian thinker of the second century[22]).

At the same time, Augustine sets a limit on the extent to which one might have recourse to Plato. Augustine had insisted with Plato against the Manichaeans that God was not a material substance, but transcendent. Similarly, evil became in his mind the denial of what proceeds from God (see *Confessions* 5.10.20). When it came to the creation of people, however, Augustine insisted against Platonic thought that no division between soul and flesh could be made (so *City of God* 22.12). Enfleshed humanity was the only genuine humanity, and God in Christ was engaged to raise those who were of the city of God. Moreover, Augustine specifically refuted the contention of Porphyry (and Origen) that cycles of creation could be included within the entire scheme of salvation. For Augustine, the power of the resurrection within the world was already confirmed by the miracles wrought by Christ and his martyrs. He gives the example of the healings connected with the relics of St. Stephen, recently transferred to Hippo (*City of God* 22.8).

Even now, in the power of the Catholic Church, God is represented on earth, and the present Christian epoch (*Christiana tempora*) corresponds to the millennium promised in Revelation 20 (*City of God* 20.9). This age of dawning power, released in flesh by Jesus and conveyed by the Church, simply awaits the full transition into the city of God, complete with flesh itself. It is interesting that, where Origen could cite a saying of Jesus to confirm his view of the resurrection (see Matt. 22:30;

21. See Stanley Romaine Hopper, "The Anti-Manichean Writings," *A Companion to the Study of St. Augustine*, ed. R. W. Battenhouse (New York: Oxford University Press, 1969), 148–74.

22. See Jaroslav Pelikan, *The Christian Tradition: A History of the Development of Doctrine*, vol. 1: *The Emergence of the Catholic Tradition (100–600)* (Chicago: University of Chicago Press, 1971), 123–32.

Mark 12:25; Luke 20:36), Augustine has to qualify the meaning of the same saying (*City of God* 22.18):

> They will be equal to angels in immortality and happiness, not in flesh, nor indeed in resurrection, which the angels had no need of, since they could not die. So the Lord said that there would be no marriage in the resurrection, not that there would be no women.

In all of this, Augustine is straining, although he is usually a less convoluted interpreter of Scripture. But he is committed to what the Latin version of the Apostles' Creed promises: "the resurrection of the flesh" and all that implies. He therefore cannot follow Origen's exegesis.

There is a double irony here. First, Origen the sophisticated allegorist seems much simpler to follow in his exegesis of Jesus' teaching than Augustine, the incomparable preacher. Second, Augustine's discussion of such issues as the fate of fetuses in the resurrection sounds remarkably like the Sadducees' hypothesis, which Jesus argues against in the relevant passage from the Synoptic Gospels.

Augustine is well aware, as was Origen before him, that Paul speaks of a "spiritual body" and acknowledges that "I suspect that all utterance published concerning it is rash." And yet he can be quite categorical that flesh must be involved somehow: "the spiritual flesh will be subject to spirit, but it will still be flesh, not spirit; just as the carnal spirit was subject to the flesh, but was still spirit, not flesh" (*City of God* 22.21). Such is Augustine's conviction that flesh has become the medium of salvation now and hereafter. As in the case of Irenaeus, the denial of a thoroughly abstract teaching leads to the assertion of greater literalism than may have been warranted.

Conclusion

Not only within the New Testament, but through the centuries of discussion which the key figures cited here reflect, Christianity represents itself as a religion of human regeneration. Humanity is regarded, not simply as a quality which God values, but as the very center of human being in the image of God.

That center is so precious to God, it is the basis upon which it is possible for human beings to enter the kingdom of God, both now and eschatologically.

The medium in which that ultimate transformation is to take place is a matter of debate. Regenerated people might be compared to angels (so Jesus), to Jesus in his resurrection (so Paul), to spiritual bodies (so Origen), and to spiritualized flesh (so Augustine). But in all of these analyses of how we are to be transformed into the image of Christ in order to apprehend that humanity which is in the image and likeness of God (see Gen. 1:27), there is a fundamental consensus. Jesus is claimed — implicitly or explicitly — as the agency by which this transformation is accomplished.

He might be the mediator of divine humanity to us because he is the teacher by whom the message of our regeneration arrives (as in Jesus' own saying), because he is a Pauline new Adam (bearing the promise of new people after him), because he is Origen's Son of God in heaven, or because he is Augustine's Son of God on earth and in history. Both the agreement and the disagreement of these theologies make it plain that the priority of Christian faith is not to determine in advance what the medium of our regeneration is to be, but rather to identify that Jesus through whom our regeneration is in fact to be realized. That identification — not of Jesus in history, but of Jesus in his divine aspect — is the key to how we are now in the presence of God, in the kingdom of God, and of how we one day will be in that presence, that kingdom.

5

Prayer through Jesus in the Circles of James, Peter, Stephen, and Paul

The Son of Man and the Circle of James

Until a few years ago, it was widely agreed that when the phrase "the Son of Man" is applied to Jesus in the Gospels, the point is to identify him as the messiah. But today, some scholars vigorously *deny* that Jesus used the phrase to make any theological claim about himself.[1] Instead, they say the phrase just referred to any human being, one person among all the others. The battle is on between those who see the phrase as messianic ("the Son of Man" with capitals) and those who see the phrase as general (any "son of man" with firmly lower-case letters).

The disagreement among publications in the field is likely to cause confusion, and there is a large number of books to choose from. (Harvard's on-line catalogue lists some seventy-two books, not to mention articles, which are primarily dedicated to this subject.) General readers and specialists alike can ask the same question which a crowd asks in John 12:34, and with the same sort of exasperation, "Who is this Son of Man?"

Principal Texts and Interpretations at Issue

Jesus refers to the Son of Man many times in the earliest Gospels (Matthew, Mark, and Luke), and *Jesus is the only person who*

---

1. In North American discussion, this position is best represented by Douglas R. A. Hare, *The Son of Man Tradition* (Minneapolis: Fortress, 1990).

uses the phrase in those sources. It is presented as a part of his characteristic speech; he uses "the Son of Man" more frequently than any other reference (including "Son of God" and "Messiah") to explain who he is. That is the reason the scholarly dispute has been as heated as it has been. The debate concerns whether Jesus saw himself as an exceptional figure or as just one example of humanity at large.

There are three groups of sayings throughout the Synoptic Gospels which associate Jesus with "the Son of Man." One group speaks of his authority (for example, to forgive sins),[2] another group relates to the way people treat the Son of Man (typically, without respect) and how he is to suffer and then be vindicated.[3] The third group refers to his triumphant arrival in judgment at the end of all things as eschatological redeemer.[4] Obviously, that is a very wide range of meaning, so it is understandable that the issue of the original meaning of the phrase is as contested as it is.

But the question of the original meaning of the phrase will be answered only when we can point to what Jesus said that brought about the rich associations of the Son of Man's authority, his suffering, and his triumph. Jesus' sayings as we have them in the Gospels were generated within Jesus' movement in the period between its beginnings in Galilee and the Graeco-Roman congregations which produced the Gospels we can read today. We have to allow for the development of meanings over time, but finally the meaning which best explains how all the others emerged is most likely to have been the meaning of Jesus.

---

2. See Matthew 9:6/Mark 2:10/Luke 5:24; Matthew 12:8/Mark 2:28/Luke 6:5; Luke 6:22; 9:56; Matthew 12:32/Luke 12:10; Matthew 12:40/Luke 11:30; Matthew 13:37; Matthew 16:13; Matthew 17:9/Mark 9:9; Matthew 18:11/Luke 19:10; Matthew 20:28/Mark 10:45.

3. See Matthew 8:20/Luke 9:58; Matthew 16:21/Mark 8:31/Luke 9:22; Matthew 11:19/Luke 7:34; Matthew 17:12/Mark 9:12; Matthew 17:22–23/Mark 9:31/Luke 9:44; Matthew 20:18–19/Mark 10:33–34/Luke 18:31–33; Matthew 26:2; Matthew 26:24/Mark 14:21/Luke 22:22; Matthew 26:45/Mark 14:41; Luke 22:48; 24:7.

4. See Matthew 10:23; 13:41; 16:27–28; Mark 8:38/Luke 9:26; Luke 12:8; 17:22; Matthew 24:27/Luke 17:24; Luke 18:8; Matthew 24:30–31/Mark 13:26–27/Luke 21:27; Luke 21:36; Matthew 24:37/Luke 17:26; Matthew 24:39/Luke 17:30; Matthew 24:44/Luke 12:40; Matthew 25:31; Matthew 26:64/Mark 14:62/Luke 22:69.

One reason for the old agreement on a consistently messianic understanding of the phrase was that the book of Daniel clearly identifies the agent of final judgment as being human, "one like a son of man" (Dan. 7:13–14):

> I saw in visions of the night, and behold,
> with clouds of heaven one like a son of man was coming
> and he approached the Ancient of Days [that is, God himself],
> and they [the angels in the divine court] presented him before him.
> And to him was given dominion and glory and kingdom,
> that all peoples, nations, and languages should serve him;
> his dominion is an everlasting dominion which shall not pass away,
> and his kingdom one that shall not be destroyed.

Here an angelic figure is said to be "like a son of man," in the sense of "like a human being." In fact, the latter translation is found in the New Revised Standard Version. A general quality, in other words, the quality of being human, is ascribed to the figure to whom an everlasting dominion is given.

This visionary passage appears at the literary heart of the book of Daniel, and its meaning is plain. The kingdoms of the lion, the bear, the leopard, and the beast of the terrible horns are all to be removed (7:1–12). (The probable reference is to the Assyrian, Babylonian, and Persian empires, followed by the multiple "horns" of Alexander the Great and his successors.) The one like a son of man, Israel's heavenly counterpart of the beasts, is alone to receive a kingdom which stands forever. After his vision, Daniel seeks interpretation from one of the angels in the heavenly court, "one of those standing there" (Dan. 7:16), constantly at the ready to serve the Ancient of Days. The angel was among those who had just presented the one like a son of man at the divine throne, and therefore was in an ideal position to know the significance of the vision. Daniel is told that the four beasts are four kings, and that when the Son of Man is presented to the Ancient of Days, "the saints of the most high shall receive the kingdom, and possess the kingdom for ever" (Dan. 7:17–18).

Just as the visionary angels of the previous kingdoms are beasts, the visionary angel of the final kingdom is "one like a son of man." God's will is that he, the angelic figure in the heavenly court, is to be the guarantor of the rule of the saints of the most high. The final chapter of Daniel refers explicitly to the resurrection, the only such reference in the Hebrew Bible; the events unfold when the archangel Michael arises from his place in the heavenly court (Dan. 12:1–3). As described in the book of Daniel, "one like a son of man"[5] is clearly identified as the messianic and angelic redeemer of Israel, a truly heavenly redeemer known to Israel as the archangel Michael.

The image of the messianic and angelic Son of Man in Daniel was a powerful development within the eschatological hopes of early Judaism and Christianity. In the book of Enoch, the phrase "the Son of Man" is used in order to refer to a prominent figure in the heavenly court, privileged in his position near the throne of God (see Enoch 46:1–4):

> At that place, I saw the one to whom belongs the time before time. And his head was white like wool, and there was before him another individual, whose face was like that of a human being. His countenance was full of grace like that of one among the holy angels. And I asked the one — from among the angels — who was going with me..., "Who is this...?" And he answered me and said to me, "This is the Son of Man to whom belongs righteousness, and with whom righteousness dwells. And he will open all the hidden storerooms; for the Lord of the Spirits has chosen him, and he is destined to be victorious before the Lord of Spirits in eternal uprightness. This Son of Man whom you have seen is the one who will remove the kings and the mighty ones from their comfortable seats and the strong ones from their thrones.

The Son of Man was a well-known designation by the time the book was composed. The reference was to the Son of Man whom Daniel had spoken of, and the imagery of the passage

---

5. See the similar phrase in Daniel 10:16, 18; in both cases, the reference is also angelic.

in Enoch 46 simply develops what is already in Daniel 7. But it is not certain that the usage is pre-Christian; the portion of the book of Enoch with which we are concerned has not been found at Qumran (although other sections have been) and may date from a period well after Jesus. Similarly, the vision of "one like a son of man" in Revelation 1:12–20 is a way of depicting Jesus after his resurrection by speaking of his heavenly status in terms borrowed from Daniel 7. But that obviously does not prove how Jesus himself used the phrase.

Taken together, the evidence of Daniel, Enoch, and the Revelation of John demonstrate that some people thought God's final judgment would be accomplished with "one like a son of man." Just such a figure of final judgment is in view when Jesus warns his hearers in a well-known saying:

> Whoever is ashamed of me and of my words in this adulterous and sinful generation, the Son of Man will be ashamed of him, when he comes in his father's glory with his holy angels. (Mark 8:38)

That saying appears in Mark and derives from the tradition of Peter, which was shaped into the form of a gospel by the time Peter met Paul in the year 35 C.E. (so Gal. 1:18–20). That early attestation of the saying is joined by the source of Jesus' sayings known as "Q," which was circulating in Aramaic at the same time. "Q" presents a similar (but distinct) form of the saying (best represented in Luke 12:8–9, but also reflected in a different form in Matt. 10:32–33).

Here Jesus himself picks up the image of the Son of Man as found in the book of Daniel. That Son of Man, he says, will finally and definitively insist upon the truth of Jesus' own teaching. The saying is attested in the three Synoptic Gospels, in sources which take us back to within a few years of the crucifixion and resurrection of Jesus.

The only possible argument against accepting the authenticity of the saying is that Jesus cannot have claimed so much authority for himself. A publication of the "Jesus Seminar" makes that assumption.[6] In other words, a preconceived view

---

6. See R. W. Funk and R. W. Hoover, *The Five Gospels* (New York: Mac-

of what Jesus *could* have said about himself has determined the judgment of what he *did* say about himself. Several of us who have participated in the "Jesus Seminar," although we have appreciated the experience, have criticized our colleagues for voting along what seem to be ideological lines. Historical judgments should be based upon an analysis of how traditions concerning Jesus developed, not on global assumptions regarding what he should have said or could have said. A much more likely historical finding is that Jesus himself referred to the Son of Man of Daniel 7, and that the memory of that reference echoes through our sources.

The question really is not whether there is a reference to Daniel 7 within some of Jesus' sayings concerning the Son of Man. The issue is rather: given that there is reference to Daniel 7 in several of the sayings, how did the very distinct meanings of the authoritative, suffering, and triumphant Son of Man develop? A British school of thought, represented by T. W. Manson in his classic work *The Teaching of Jesus,*[7] argues that the Son of Man is a symbol of obedience. The idea is that, if one is as obedient as Jesus was, one will be vindicated. Although that is indeed a general theme of the Gospels (see, for example, Mark 8:34–35 and parallels), it hardly explains the rich nuances of Jesus' reference to the Son of Man.

Manson's book does not take account of the suggestion which had been made by Rudolf Bultmann. Bultmann called attention to the fact that, in Mark 8:38, Jesus refers to himself and to the Son of Man *as distinct figures.* It was his idea that Jesus referred to the Son of Man of Daniel 7 as the divine confirmation of his teaching by a heavenly figure, the Danielic "one like a son of man."[8] As in the case of many great ideas in

---

millan, 1993), 80. The phrase is actually translated "the son of Adam," which is hardly accurate.

7. First published in 1931 by the Cambridge University Press; a second edition appeared in 1935. There have been many reprints. See p. 227, where he asserts that the Son of Man "stands for the manifestation of the Kingdom of God on earth in a people wholly devoted to their heavenly King."

8. This interpretation was later developed by H. E. Tödt, *The Son of Man in the Synoptic Tradition,* trans. D. M. Barton (Westminster: Philadelphia, 1965), 40–46. For a lucid statement by Bultmann himself, see *Theology of the New Testament,* trans. K. Grobel (New York: Scribner's, 1951), 1:29. The idea was already evident in his *Jesus* (Berlin: Deutsche Bibliothek, 1926), 196–200, trans-

scholarship, Bultmann's is simple, and yet it has profound implications. *When Jesus refers to the Son of Man, he does not have only himself in mind, but is thinking of the figure in the heavenly court described in Daniel.* That Son of Man, Jesus said many times, would vindicate his teaching.

So why is there any doubt about Jesus' meaning? If he referred to the messianic Son of Man of Daniel 7, the only real question would be: did he claim himself to be that figure, or did he think of the Son of Man as an angel in the heavenly court? Here we have to pause in discussing Bultmann's insight, because he did not take up the question of what "Son of Man" would have meant in Aramaic.[9] And it is on the basis of the Aramaic phrase (*bar 'enasha*) that some scholars have asserted that there is no christological meaning in "the Son of Man" at all.

Great Semitists of the turn of the century such as Julius Wellhausen and Gustaf Dalman established that "son of man" may mean "a person," a generic example of humanity, just as the phrase "that man" (*hahu' gabra'*) can refer to "a certain person," meaning "I."[10] Now there is also a big difference in saying "a person" ("a son of man") and saying "I" ("that man"). "Son of man" refers to people in a generic way, while "that man" designates a particular individual, and probably only that person.

The point should be kept in mind, because the confusion between the two idioms has muddled the discussion of Aramaic meaning since a major contribution by Geza Vermes.[11] Vermes realizes that "son of man" is at base a generic idiom. It is well

lated as *Jesus and the Word,* trans. L. P. Smith and E. H Lantero (New York: Scribner's, 1958), 214–19, and see his *History of the Synoptic Tradition,* trans. J. Marsh (Oxford: Blackwell, 1963), 151ff.; *Die Erforschung der synoptischen Evangelien* (Giessen: Töpelmann, 1925), 29–36.

9. For the form and meaning of the phrase in the first century, see Joseph A. Fitzmyer, "The New Testament Title 'Son of Man' Philologically Considered," in *A Wandering Aramean: Collected Aramaic Essays* (Chico, Calif.: Scholars Press, 1979), 143–60.

10. They are cited in Manson, *The Teaching of Jesus,* 217–18.

11. See *Jesus the Jew* (Philadelphia: Fortress, 1981), 160–91. Vermes in fact accepts some of the criticism which has built up since the time of the paper on which his chapter is based (which he delivered in 1965), but he does not actually incorporate the necessary changes into his presentation.

represented, not only in Aramaic sources, but in the Hebrew Bible (see Ps. 8:4):

> What is man that you are mindful of him,
> and son of man that you have regard for him?

The psalmist obviously includes himself in the category of human beings for whom God's care comes as a miracle. But to speak of the phrase as a "circumlocution" for "I" (as Vermes does) is misleading, because the psalmist is not talking about himself first of all, but of people in general.

The confusion becomes important, because Vermes attempts to derive *all* Jesus' usages of the phrase "son of man" from what he inaccurately calls a circumlocution. As Vermes sees it, all the time, Jesus was just talking about himself as an ordinary person, when mistakes in translation and interpretation resulted in his being portrayed as the "Son of Man" in Daniel 7. From Jesus the local teacher we move to Jesus the messiah, all by means of a series of linguistic and exegetical errors!

There is no doubt but that Jesus *did* use the Aramaic idiom "son of man" in its usual generic sense, as may be seen in another saying from "Q" (Luke 9:58/Matt. 8:20, see also *Thomas*, saying 86):

> The foxes have holes, and the birds of heaven nests,
> but the son of man has nowhere to lay his head.

The saying applies in context, not simply to Jesus (as a circumlocution would), but to homeless disciples generally, and it carries with it a resonant sympathy for homeless people as a whole. "The son of man" here can *not* mean "me, myself, I: and no one else." Others are included with the speaker, as in Psalm 8:4.

At least we can now suggest that a proper understanding of Aramaic usage links Jesus' experience with the experience of those who would follow him. That would explain one of the categories explained at the beginning of this article: the treatment of the Son of Man, and his suffering.[12] But after so many

---

12. An especially helpful article in that regard is John W. Bowker, "The Son of Man," *Journal of Theological Studies* 28 (1977): 19–48.

years of intense discussion that seems scant progress. The crucial point is: how can we understand *both* the generic and the angelic/messianic meanings of "Son of Man"?

The New Solution: The Son of Man as Human and Heavenly

The solution is to be found by becoming more precise than much discussion has been. Jesus is actually not quoted as referring to "son of man" in general, but to "*the* Son of Man." Although the usage has sometimes been described as barbaric, it is in fact straightforward Greek. C. F. D. Moule, one of the finest exegetes and grammarians of the New Testament which Great Britain has produced in this century, has pointed out that specifying "the" Son of Man simply refers to a well-known usage of the phrase.[13] The phrase "*the* Son of Man" works much the way we say "*the* White House": in theory, there might be many sons of men and white houses, but only the one White House, the one Son of Man is at issue.

"The Son of Man" at issue must be the figure of Daniel 7, Israel's advocate in the heavenly court, the angel identified later in the book as Michael.[14] Jesus' reference to the Son of Man, insistently with the word "the," indicates that the angelic figure of Danielic usage was very much a part of his own idiom. There is no reasonable way of denying that Jesus spoke of the Son of Man in this way.

But the angelic/messianic reference of the Son of Man does not easily explain Jesus' generic usages of the phrase. The old dilemma has returned to haunt us: one solution takes account of a messianic meaning and leaves the generic aspect unexplained, while another solution reduces the generic sayings to banal truisms, while dismissing messianic sayings as Christian

---

13. See "Neglected Features in the Problem of the Son of Man," *Essays in New Testament Interpretation* (Cambridge: Cambridge University Press, 1982), 75–90.

14. Because Moule follows Manson's interpretation, he does not pursue the angelic meaning developed in Daniel. For examples of the approach I am taking, see Frederick Houk Borsch, *The Son of Man in Myth and History* (Philadelphia: Westminster, 1967), 137–45, and David Catchpole, "The Angelic Son of Man in Luke 12:8," *Novum Testamentum* 24 (1982): 255–65. Taken together, Moule, Borsch, and Catchpole represent the genuine progress which has taken place in discussion since the time of Manson.

inventions. If one of these solutions (or their many variations) could claim to accord with the history of the evolution of the traditions within the Gospels, that would lend it some support. But both the usages are early (as we have seen), and both die out of frequent usage after the period of the New Testament. Simply put: Jesus obviously was smart enough to use the phrase in both ways, and scholars have not yet figured out how to put the two together.

For most of critical scholarship, Jesus is a rational teacher who wished to convey a single, prosaic meaning. The current debate is between "conservatives," who want to see the Son of Man as only messianic, and "liberals," who want to see him as only generic. In fact, both adhere to the nineteenth-century liberal presupposition of rationality as the primary motivation in human affairs. Their disagreement is a sideshow compared to the basic question: can we understand Jesus at all if we make the liberal assumption that he was rational by our standards of rationality? The sayings concerning the Son of Man answer that question clearly and unequivocally. We simply cannot understand them if we assume Jesus' meaning was prosaic.

The passage in John 12:34, where the crowd expresses its exasperation (and perhaps ours), actually points to the need to see Jesus' usage as more than prosaic. When Jesus speaks of the exaltation of the Son of Man, the crowd replies impatiently:

> We have heard from the law that the messiah lives forever, and how do you say that the Son of Man must be exalted? Who is this, the Son of Man?

They understand "messiah" and they understand "Son of Man," and *for that reason* they do not understand the messianic Son of Man. John's Gospel is here showing us what is difficult to grasp about the Son of Man, and how to get over our confusion. The crowd assumes (as do liberal critics) that the Son of Man must be either generic or messianic, while Jesus uses the phrase in both those dimensions. He operates in the realm of poetry, not prose.

Jesus was a master of the parable, the comparison (*matla'* in Aramaic). Comparative speech was his particular strength; he could portray the kingdom of God in terms of growing seed, a woman making bread, or a merchant out to close an attractive deal. The point of his parables was that you could understand the kingdom in terms of such realities, and that such ordinary activities found their true meanings in the reality of the kingdom. Jesus' characteristic activity was to eat with people, and those meals were themselves enacted parables: celebrations of the festivity of the kingdom of God.[15] Basic human activities were intimately connected with the ultimate kingdom of God: that was the theme of Jesus' ministry, and he defined the purity of Israel in terms of people's readiness to respond to the opportunities of the kingdom.

If we appreciate that Jesus genuinely related his own activity and the activities of those around him to the kingdom of God, then we are in a position to appreciate his sayings concerning the Son of Man. Who can have insight into the ways of the divine king, seated upon his heavenly throne? To anyone who took Daniel 7 seriously as a depiction of that throne, the answer would be that the Son of Man of that vision provides access to the mystery of the divine kingship. When Jesus preached that the kingdom of God was celebrated by his ministry, he claimed to have an insight into the ways of heaven. That insight, Jesus went on to claim, will be warranted by the Son of Man in heaven, "when he comes in his father's glory with his holy angels" (Mark 8:38). He and the Son of Man together were the agents of God's final intervention in human affairs.

Now we may come back to Bultmann's insight. He was right to say that Jesus speaks not only of himself when he refers to the Son of Man. But we need to correct Bultmann's picture. *Because Jesus, a son of man on earth, saw himself as paired with the Danielic Son of Man in heaven, there is a sliding scale of reference. Sometimes he thinks more of the one, at other times more of the other. This combined, poetic usage is Jesus' own invention: the Son of Man as human and heavenly.*

Sometimes Jesus referred more to himself as the Son of Man, as when he complained that he (and others, including his followers) had no place to lodge, while foxes and birds did. At

---

15. See Bruce Chilton, "The Eucharist — Exploring Its Origins," *Bible Review* 10, no. 6 (December 1994): 36–43.

other times, he referred more to the majesty of the Danielic vision, when he thought of the final judgment in which the Son of Man was to be the agent. But at every point, the two references illuminated one another, because the Son of Man was for Jesus both human and heavenly.[16] The reality of the kingdom was attested in heaven and on earth, in both cases by the Son of Man.

When Jesus is permitted to cease being a rational teacher of reasonable truth and to become the paradoxical, poetic rabbi he more truly was, his message becomes clearer. His teaching is more challenging when it is so understood; it may be unbelievable to many people, but it is nonetheless clearer within its historical context. *Jesus asserted that God was acting as king, and he implicitly claimed that he alone knew how.* His teaching and his activity were designed to make his announcement concerning the kingdom as public as possible. That desire to publicize the kingdom is what caused Jesus to send his disciples out in his name, the one aspect of his ministry which seems to make him unlike other rabbis of his period.

Jesus' reference to "the Son of Man" makes explicit what his preaching about the kingdom of God always implied. He claimed that he, a person (a *bar 'enasha*) like any other, enjoyed access to the heavenly court through the angelic figure who was like a person (*kebar 'enasha*). The Son of Man of Daniel 7 confirmed the words of the Son of Man who spoke to his disciples. Jesus' claim was not that he was identical with the Son of Man, but that he was intimate with the Son of Man. It was a claim which was no more and no less audacious than his assertion that the kingdom of God had arrived with his ministry. The Jesus of history is not what the old liberalism would desire, a skilled interpreter of timeless truth, but a demanding poet, seized by a prophetic vision which overcame him and those around him with its power.

---

16. For further exegesis, bibliography, and discussion, see Bruce Chilton, "The Son of Man: Human and Heavenly," *The Four Gospels: 1992*, Festschrift Frans Neirynck, ed. F. van Segbroeck, C. M. Tuckett, G. van Belle, J. Verheyden, BETL 100 (Leuven, 1992), 203–18, also published in *Approaches to Ancient Judaism: Religious and Theological Studies*, South Florida Studies in the History of Judaism 81, ed. J. Neusner (Atlanta: Scholars Press, 1993), 97–114.

The two themes, the kingdom of God and the Son of Man, imply one another. The kingdom is the public theme of Jesus' ministry, what was spoken of openly and fully to anyone who would hear. The Son of Man was the esoteric theme, the explanation to those who responded to the message of the kingdom of how Jesus could know what he did. Many rabbis spoke of the visionary reality of God's throne, which they usually referred to as the "chariot," in the manner of Ezekiel 1.[17] The vision of Daniel 7 is in part inspired by the passage in Ezekiel, which even speaks of a human appearance with the throne (Ezek. 1:26). Jesus claimed that access to the heavenly Son of Man gave him, as human Son of Man, the insight which he displayed into the throne of God.

Jesus offered his contemporaries new insight into God as king on the basis that his teaching concerning the kingdom would be confirmed by the Son of Man in heaven. That special relationship between Jesus and the Son of Man permeates Jesus' teaching and accounts for the large number of sayings concerning the Son of Man in the Gospels.

Of course, the insight into heaven which Jesus taught was not just a repetition of what any rabbi might have taught. His teaching about the kingdom of God and the Son of Man was distinctive. He explained why he knew about such matters, while other rabbis did not (Matt. 11:27; Luke 10:22):

Everything has been entrusted to me by my Father, and nobody is familiar with the Son except the Father, and nobody is familiar with the Father except the Son, and the one to whom the Son chooses to reveal him.

This "Son" knows about the kingdom of God and is especially associated with the Son of Man who sits by the throne of God. This "Son" is uniquely related to God on the basis of what the Father reveals to him: he is the Son of God by virtue of that revelation. Jesus' claim to divine Sonship is part and parcel of his teaching concerning the kingdom of God and the Son of Man.

---

17. See Gershom G. Scholem, *Major Trends in Jewish Mysticism* (New York: Schocken, 1969), 40–79.

The Son of Man after the Resurrection

Jesus' death grievously disappointed the hopes of those who responded to his message of the kingdom. But the disappointment was momentary for some of them. The resurrection produced a conviction among the disciples that Jesus was alive and that he had been vindicated by God. He had been exalted to the heavenly throne of which he had spoken.

An early authority who was crucial in the development of that conviction was James, Jesus' brother. He was a key witness of the risen Jesus according to the testimony of Paul, the earliest writer to speak of Jesus' resurrection (see 1 Cor. 15:7). The New Testament itself does not record an appearance to James, but the *Gospel according to the Hebrews* does. There, Jesus assures his brother that "the Son of Man has been raised from among those who sleep."[18] The authority of James, it seems, was a key force in the complete identification between Jesus and the figure of Daniel 7 after the resurrection. Once that identification was made, it was natural for Jesus' own sayings to be recast to speak consistently of his own authority, of his own treatment and suffering, of his own vindication. But his original parabolic speech still shines through the texts as they have been received.

So who is this Son of Man? The Son of Man was Jesus' way of talking about himself as a person who had access to the very throne of God, the place of another angelic person. Jesus took a classic passage from the Bible (Daniel 7), blended it with an Aramaic idiom of his time, and related himself to the result. That was his characteristic manner of dealing with the Scripture.[19] He was not known for simply citing texts or commenting upon them, but for reshaping them in the light of the kingdom.

Jesus has been called charismatic, but that vague term has been trivialized in recent discussion. What made Jesus stand out among rabbis from Galilee was that he was a religious visionary, a seer of the kingdom and of the Son of Man, who

---

18. See Jerome's quotation of the passage in *Famous Men* 2. For translations, see E. Hennecke and W. Schneemelcher, *New Testament Apocrypha*, trans. R. McL. Wilson (London: SCM, 1973), or R. J. Miller, *The Complete Gospels* (Sonoma, Calif.: Polebridge, 1994).

19. See Bruce Chilton, *A Galilean Rabbi and His Bible: Jesus' Use of the Interpreted Scripture of His Time* (Wilmington: Glazier, 1984).

claimed implicitly and explicitly that he approached the throne of God. Any person can accept Jesus' teaching (in any time) by making that vision one's own; whether one calls oneself "conservative" or "liberal" in the process is beside the point of faith. Jesus was either right or wrong about the kingdom, right or wrong about the Son of Man; for those who believe he was right, it is natural to join his brother James in identifying the risen Jesus completely with that Son of Man, linked with God on his throne. But whatever one's response to Jesus' claims, it is perfectly possible to understand him in his historical setting.

The challenge of understanding the Gospels involves making reasoned inferences in regard to the teaching of Jesus and the interpretations of his first followers. By tracing them, we can understand how meanings interweaved with one another, in order to generate the texts which are open before us. The fabric of the Gospels was produced by the distinctive faiths of those who were involved in composing them. "The Son of Man" is a thread which starts with Jesus: originally, Jesus developed an intriguing juxtaposition between his own humanity and the heavenly person at God's right hand. Woven together with the faith in Jesus' resurrection, the fabric of the Gospels presents Jesus himself as that heavenly figure, the messianic agent of final vindication.

Once it has been appreciated that the resurrection resulted in identifying Jesus and the Son of Man, the characteristic piety of James becomes explicable. James's devotion to the Temple has already been discussed in the first two volumes of our series Christianity and Judaism — the Formative Categories.[20] Hegesippus — as cited by Eusebius (see *History* II.23.1–18) — characterizes James, Jesus' brother, as the person who exercised immediate control of the church in Jerusalem. Although Peter had initially gathered a group of Jesus' followers in Jerusalem, his interests and activities further afield left the way open for James to become the natural head of the community there. That change, and political changes in Jerusalem itself, made the Temple the effective center of the local community of Jesus'

---

20. See especially chapter 6 in volume 2, "The Israel of James, the Community of Q, and Peter."

followers. James practiced a careful and idiosyncratic purity in the interests of worship in the Temple. He abstained from wine and animal flesh, did not cut his hair or beard, and forsook oil and bathing. According to Hegesippus, those special practices gave him access even to the sanctuary. Josephus reports he was killed in the Temple c. 62 at the instigation of the high priest Ananus during the interregnum of the Roman governors Festus and Albinus (*Antiquities* 20.9.1 §§ 197–203). Hegesippus gives a more circumstantial, less politically informed, account of the martyrdom.

In addition to the sort of close association with the Temple which could and did result in conflict with the authorities there, the circle of James is expressly claimed in Acts to have exerted authority as far away as Antioch, by means of emissaries who spoke Greek (Acts 15:13–35).[21] James's devotion to the Temple is also reflected in Acts 21. When Paul arrives in Jerusalem, James and the presbyters with him express concern at the rumor that Paul is telling Jews who live among the gentiles not to circumcise. Their advice is for Paul to demonstrate his piety by purifying himself, paying the expenses of four men under a vow, and entering the Temple with them (Acts 21:17–26). The result is a disastrous misunderstanding. Paul is accused of introducing "Greeks" into the Temple, a riot ensues, and Paul himself is arrested (21:27–36). James is not mentioned again in Acts, but Hegesippus's description shows his devotion to the Temple did not wane.

James's devotion to the Temple and his devotion to Jesus were coextensive. In each case, the focus was on the throne of God. His throne on earth was in Jerusalem, where James continued to offer worship and to insist on that purity throughout the Church which made that worship both possible and acceptable to God. That Temple was the doorway to God's throne in heaven, much as in the vision of the prophet in Isaiah 6. And in the vision of James, the Son of Man associated with that throne

---

21. The particulars of the dispute (with both Pauline and Petrine understandings of purity) will not detain us here, because they have been discussed at some length in chapter 4, "The Bible in the Church," in volume 1 of our series Christianity and Judaism — the Formative Categories.

was none other than Jesus. Devotion to him *and* to the Temple together constituted the effective worship of God.

The Spirit in the Circle of Peter

Within the book of Acts, Peter's ministry is the pivot around which the story of the Church turns. He is the person who directs the preaching of the gospel to non-Jews, while Paul is still a recently converted persecutor of disciples. The great scene which represents the most momentous development in the history of the Church comes at the center of Acts. Before it, action focuses on Jerusalem; after it, the story chiefly concerns what happens in the wider world. The scene at issue, the sequence of events involving Peter in the house of Cornelius (Acts 10), illustrates how in the circle of Peter it was understood that the Spirit of God had become available by means of Jesus.

Cornelius himself is portrayed as a Roman soldier, a centurion of the cohort called Italica. He is, then, a gentile of the gentiles; non-Jewish by both descent and profession. Nonetheless, he is described as pious and "fearing God," a righteous person with his household, faithful to the covenant with Israel in all but circumcision (see especially Acts 10:2, 4, 22, 31, 35).[22] In a vision in Caesarea (a Roman headquarters for administration), Cornelius is assured that his prayers and his alms have been looked on favorably by God, and he is directed to send to Joppa for Simon Peter (10:1–8).

While emissaries from Cornelius are on the way to Joppa, Peter goes up on the roof of the house to pray near noon. He there has an extraordinary and disturbing vision. Feeling hungry, he has an ecstatic vision of a great sheet being lowered from heaven, and it is filled with four-footed animals, reptiles, and birds. A voice says, "Arise, Peter, slaughter and eat," and he refuses (in words reminiscent of Ezek. 4:14). But a voice again says, "What God has cleansed, you will not defile" (see Acts 10:9–15). After a repetition of this experience, Peter is directed

---

22. The social location of Cornelius is assessed in the second volume of our trilogy, chapter 5, "Jesus and the Absence of Israel."

by the Spirit to return downstairs and to go with people who have been sent for him (Acts 10:16–23).

When they finally meet in Caesarea, in Cornelius's house, Peter explains that in the vision "God has shown me that I should not call any human being profane or unclean" (Acts 10:28) and that as a result he has broken with his custom of avoiding non-Jews. Cornelius also relates his experience, and its consequence: "now therefore we are all in the presence of God to hear all that has been laid upon you by the Lord" (Acts 10:33). Peter then recounts a summary of primitive Christian preaching which accords with the general order and content of the Synoptic Gospels (Acts 10:34–43). That summary is a valuable indication of the nature of the initial preaching to prospective converts in the earliest phase of the Church's life, and such concise outlines of instruction in oral form were probably the basis on which the written Gospels later evolved.

While he was still speaking, the Holy Spirit came upon those who listened to Peter, as attested by their praising God in tongues other than their own (Acts 10:44, 46). Despite the astonishment of "those of the circumcision" who would restrict baptism to those who were already circumcised (Acts 10:45), Peter arranges for them to be baptized in the name of Jesus Christ (Acts 10:48). His argument is that the water of baptism cannot be withheld from those who received the Spirit as the apostles themselves had (Acts 10:47).

Peter defends his baptisms in the house of Cornelius on the basis of his vision in the course of a dispute with those who argued that circumcision was a requirement of adherence to the movement (Acts 11:1–18). He also cites his activity among non-Jews at a later point in the context of what has come to be called the Apostolic Council (Acts 15:7–11). Throughout, the position of Peter appears to have been consistent: God may make, and has made, eschatological exceptions to the usual practice of purity. Those exceptions include the acceptance of uncircumcised men in baptism, and fellowship with them.[23]

Our present concern is not with the overall policy which

---

23. This aspect of the story is developed in chapter 6 of the second volume of our trilogy, "The Israel of James, the Community of Q, and Peter."

Peter's vision occasions. That has been the focus in the first two volumes of our trilogy. Now the issue is distinct: what is the Petrine understanding of prayer which the narrative of Peter's visit in the household of Cornelius conveys? The supposition is not that the story as a whole should be read as historical, but that in the presentation of Luke-Acts it does reflect what C. K. Barrett has called "a decisive step, perhaps the decisive step, in the expansion of Christianity into the non-Jewish world":

> The theological interpretation of this step is hinted at in 10:47; 11:18, and given explicitly in 15:7–9. Its foundation is that there is no respect of persons with God (10:34); non-Jews are welcomed into the people of God, and the only sign of their initiation is baptism. They are not required to be circumcised and, it appears, Peter not only baptized but ate with them (11:3; cf. 10:48). That he did in fact eat with uncircumcised gentile Christians is confirmed by Gal. 2:12 (he ate with them until threatened from without).[24]

The entire story seems to stem from Caesarea as an account of the founding of the church there[25] and in that sense only indirectly concerns Peter. Indeed, the entire point of the passage is that Peter, Cornelius, and his household operate collectively as instruments of God's Spirit.

Churches which accepted the gospel preached by Peter saw Jesus as a new Moses and a new Elijah, which is how he is portrayed in the Petrine story of the Transfiguration (see Mark 9:2–10 and parallels[26]). Moses' authority was not simply a matter of the assent he could command, but derived also from his ability to direct Spirit from him to his followers. Seventy elders of Israel receive from the spirit which rests upon Moses (Num. 11:16–17) and Joshua's reception of Spirit is linked to the fact that Moses laid hands on him (Deut. 34:9). Similarly, Elisha as-

---

24. C. K. Barrett, *The Acts of the Apostles*, International Critical Commentary (Edinburgh: T. & T. Clark, 1994), 495.

25. So Barrett, in *Acts of the Apostles*, 496–97.

26. The passage is discussed in chapter 4 of the first volume of the trilogy, "The Bible in the Church."

sumes that Elijah is in a position to provide a double share of the Spirit which is upon him (so 2 Kings 2:9).

All these scenes find their resonance in the Gospels. Jesus sends out seventy disciples in Luke (10:1–17), and breathes the Holy Spirit upon his disciples in John so that they might have the power to forgive sins (20:22–23). The principal scene of apostolic empowerment, of course, appears in Acts, where the events at Pentecost are interpreted by Peter as God's decision to pour out his Spirit upon the followers of Jesus (Acts 2:1–36). Although the last scene mentioned has been heavily influenced by a universalizing theology whose origin will concern us below, when we speak of the circle of Stephen, the fact remains that it enshrines a key element of Petrine teaching. Jesus, raised from the dead and exalted to the right hand of God, is said by Peter to have poured out the Spirit which can be seen and heard by anyone who pays attention to Jesus' inspired disciples (Acts 2:32–33).

Where the focus of the resurrection in the circle of James was on Jesus as exalted to the position of the Son of Man, present in the heavenly court, the circle of Peter emphasized Jesus' authority from that position to bring about a new effusion of Spirit. The assumption of the narrative concerning Cornelius and Peter (in that order!) is that Spirit is accessible to them both, assuming the integrity of their prayer. For such prayers Cornelius is told he is heard, and the generosity of his actions goes hand in hand with them (so Acts 10:4). Peter has already been attested in the narrative which precedes as a man of much prayer (so Acts 1:14; 2:42; 3:1; 6:4) and no personal property at all (so Acts 2:42–47; 4:32–5:11). These marks of integrity, fully consonant with the last petition of the Lord's Prayer (as discussed in the last chapter), accord with the capacity of Cornelius and Peter both to experience and rightly to interpret the Spirit of God.

We may contrast the Petrine presentation of the risen Jesus with the reputation of Jesus' younger contemporary, Hillel, among many rabbis. Hillel was held in such high esteem that he was thought worthy to receive the Holy Spirit. That estimate appears all the more exalted, but also strangely wistful, when it is borne in mind that the rabbis held that the Spirit had been withdrawn since the time of the last prophets of Scripture.[27] These motifs are drawn together in a most exciting manner in Tosefta Sotah 13:3:

> Until the dead live, namely, Haggai, Zechariah, and Malachi, the latter prophets, the Holy Spirit has ceased from Israel. Yet even so, they made them hear *bath qol*. An example: the sages gathered at the house of Guria in Jericho, and they heard a *bath qol* saying, There is here a man who is predestined for the Holy Spirit, except that his generation is not righteous enough for that. And they put their eyes on Hillel the elder, and when he died, they said of him, Woe the meek man, Woe, the faithful disciple of Ezra.

On first acquaintance, this haggadah is simply — and evocatively — poignant of rabbinic virtue. There is an apparent naïveté in the way the passage begins with a general statement, concerning the general efficacy of the angelic echo (*bath qol*), and is taken over by the particular vignette concerning Hillel. In fact, however, the rhetoric of the haggadah presses home its central theme, that the prophetic authority of a Haggai, a Zechariah, or a Malachi is now to be understood as reflected — if only dimly — in the succession to Hillel the elder.

Hillel is not overtly designated as worthy of the Holy Spirit by the angelic echo alone, but is so identified jointly by the deflected voice of the heavenly court *and* the sages gathered in Jericho. The two operate together, because authority is now a matter of consensus, not merely of charismatic endowment. Such an emphasis is also evident in the presentation of the Petrine story concerning Cornelius, but in a different key. Cornelius's vision and Peter's are together warranted as coming from the Spirit. The same Spirit which speaks to Peter (Acts 10:19) also empowered Jesus during his life (10:38) and is now available from the risen Jesus in baptism (10.44–48).

---

27. See Peter Schäfer, *Die Vorstellung vom heiligen Geist in der rabbinischen Literatur*, Studien zum Alten und Neuen Testament 28 (Munich: Kösel, 1972).

Two Hellenists: Stephen and Paul

Conflict in Jerusalem itself between disciples called "Hebrews" and disciples called "Hellenists" is narrated in Acts 6:1–7. The dispute concerned the distribution of resources, and it is resolved by the appointment of seven ministers to deal with the issue. All seven bear Greek names, and one is described as a proselyte from Antioch (Acts 6:5). With C. K. Barrett, it seems wise to understand that Jews from the Diaspora are at issue when the term "Hellenists" is used here.[28]

It is interesting that the seven are appointed by the laying on of hands (Acts 6:6), which is how Moses is said to have passed on the spirit to Joshua (Deut. 34:9). The number seven is also significant, since seventy was the traditional number of the nations in Judaism. "The Seven" is used as a title later in Acts (21:8), and it corresponds in the Synoptic tradition to the seven bushels which were gathered after the feeding of the four thousand (see Matt. 15:32–39; Mark 8:1–10). The symbolism of the numbers seems clear: the multiple of four refers to people all over the world, from every point of the compass, while the number seven refers to the ministry of the Church to feed them. Jesus is said to underline the symbolism and compare it to the Judaic numerology of the feeding of the five thousand (Matt. 16:5–12; Mark 8:14–21).[29]

The development of the meaning of the term "Hellenists" in Acts follows the widening of the Petrine mission. It starts with Jews from the Diaspora in Jerusalem who adhere to Jesus' movement (6:1), continues through dispute with such Jews in Jerusalem (9:29), but winds up referring to non-Jews in Antioch (11:20)! Of course, Peter himself was in an ambivalent position in regard to fellowship with non-Jews, as we have seen repeatedly during the course of our trilogy, especially in our discussion of Galatians 2. "The Hellenists," "the Seven," and Stephen in particular represent the tendency to press the

---

28. That also makes sense of the usage of the term in Acts 9:29; although Acts 11:20 would seem to refer to non-Jews. See Barrett, *Acts of the Apostles*, 308–9, 470, 549–51.

29. For further discussion of the point, see Bruce Chilton, *A Feast of Meanings: Eucharistic Theologies from Jesus through Johannine Circles*, Supplements to *Novum Testamentum* 72 (Leiden: Brill, 1994), 128–30.

Petrine conception of Spirit in the direction of a fresh, universalizing tendency.

Stephen's position is first described from the perspective of antagonists, who charge that he speaks against the Temple and the law (Acts 6:13–14, within the larger scene, 6:8–15). A very long speech of Stephen then follows in chapter 7 of Acts; indeed, Barrett has remarked that "if there is any direct relation between length and importance, this is the most important speech in Acts."[30] The strategy of the speech is to accord Moses great respect (7.20–38), but also to stress the disobedience of "our fathers" (7:39–53) *and to attack the Temple itself as a sign of disobedience* (7:47–50)! The departure from the Petrine attitude toward the Temple is manifest but is developed on the grounds of the Spirit. Stephen himself is said to be endowed with Spirit (6:3, 5, 10), and he accuses his accusers and their fathers of contradicting the Holy Spirit (7:51). What we see in the speech — in a highly developed form[31] — is the application of the authority of the Spirit in order to supplant the authority of the Temple.

The development of Stephen's position becomes even more pointed in what follows. It is said that, "full of the Holy Spirit," Stephen saw the glory of God in heaven and Jesus standing at his right hand; Stephen reports his vision as seeing "the Son of Man" (Acts 7:55–56). Although those who hear Stephen have already been described as angry (7:54), his vision is what makes them rush to stone him (7:57–60). In the context of what we have seen of the importance of "the Son of Man," their reaction is understandable. Stephen calls the heavenly throne of God in witness against what most Jews (including Peter, and most emphatically James) saw as the earthly throne of God. Stephen's challenge is all the more pointed when it is borne in mind that the principal message of the book of Daniel is that worship in the Temple is to be restored: that is to be the seal of the triumph of the saints of the most high (see Dan. 12:11–13 and 7:25–27). Their victory is assured by the Danielic Son of Man (Dan. 7:13), and just that Son of Man is invoked by Stephen in the context of an assault on such worship.

---

30. Barrett, *Acts of the Apostles*, 334.
31. As Barrett, *Acts of the Apostles*, 339, remarks, the speech "can hardly have been spoken by Stephen in the circumstances described."

The persecution which follows the martyrdom of Stephen is therefore no surprise, and the particular involvement of the authorities of the Temple was only natural (see Acts 8:1–3; 9:1–2). Although Acts exaggerates the power of the sanhedrin throughout, there can be no doubt that Stephen's position engaged the interests of the high-priesthood. Indeed, his stance was also antithetical to that of James, and it is not impossible that in the confused circumstances reflected in Acts, disciples were among those who denounced disciples for blasphemy against the Temple. In effect, the position of Stephen turned Jesus' objection against the operation of the Temple under Caiaphas into an objection in principle. The careful development of a practice of accommodation to the Temple, master-minded by Peter and perfected by James, was subverted by Stephen's stance.

As compared to Stephen's position, Paul's was somewhat moderate. Paul enjoyed the agreement of the leadership in Jerusalem, Peter and James included, that circumcision could not be required with baptism as a public mark of belief in Jesus. Where Paul parted company with Peter and James was in his insistence that the single body of Christ could not be divided by applying regulations of purity to one part of the community which did not apply to other parts of the community. A single purity applied to a single body, the company of all believers.[32] Our purpose here is not to rehearse the considerations which brought Paul to his position and into conflict with other leaders of the fledgling movement. Our point is rather that, in comparison with Stephen, Paul was quite conservative in regard to the Temple in Jerusalem.

Paul even believed he had a role to play within the service of the Temple. His preaching of the gospel is depicted in Romans 15:16 as a kind of priestly service, in that it is to result in "the offering of the nations, pleasing, sanctified in holy spirit." Contextually, Paul's characterization of his own ministry as sacrificial is associated with his "serving the saints in Jerusalem" (15:25), by means of a collection he organizes in Macedonia and

---

32. Those issues have consumed our attention in volume 1 in our trilogy (chapter 4, "The Bible in the Church") and in volume 2 (chapter 7, "The Synoptic Gospels, Paul, Hebrews, and the Revelation: Practicing the Body of Christ").

Greece for the poorer community (15:26–27). That done, Paul expects to come to Rome "in the fullness of Christ's blessing," and to proceed to Spain (vv. 28, 29), there to engage in the same priestly service (cf. v. 19). Paul's program is known conventionally as the collection[33] (following Rom. 15:26; 1 Cor. 16:1; 2, 2 Cor. 8, 9; and Gal. 2:10), and the assumption has been that the purpose of the program was purely practical: Paul agreed to provide material support in exchange for recognition by Peter, James, and John (cf. Gal. 2:9) and used priestly language as a rhetorical device.

Paul was unquestionably capable of using cultic language as metaphor. Romans 12:1 provides the example of the addressees being called to present their bodies as "a living sacrifice, holy and acceptable to God." Indeed, Romans 15:16 itself can only refer to Paul's priestly service metaphorically, as the means by which the offering of the nations might be completed. But is "the offering of the nations" itself to be taken only as a metaphor?[34] Paul might well speak here of an actual offering, provided by gentile Christians for sacrifice in Jerusalem. That meaning should not be excluded, unless the straightforward sense of the words is found to be implausible.

The hope of a climactic disclosure of divine power, signaled in the willingness of nations to worship on Mount Zion, is certainly attested within sources extant by the first century. Chief among them, from the point of view of its influence upon the New Testament, is the book of Zechariah. It has been argued that Zechariah provided the point of departure for Jesus' inclusive program of purity and forgiveness as the occasions of the kingdom.[35] Jesus is said to have mentioned the prophet by name (Matt. 23:34–36; Luke 11:49–51).[36] The book programmatically

---

33. Victor Paul Furnish, *II Corinthians*, Anchor Bible (Garden City, N.Y.: Doubleday, 1984), 408–13.

34. For an extensive consideration of the question in relation to recent discussion, see Bruce Chilton, *A Feast of Meanings: Eucharistic Theologies from Jesus through Johannine Circles*, Supplements to *Novum Testamentum* 72 (Leiden: Brill, 1994), 182–93.

35. Bruce Chilton, *The Temple of Jesus: His Sacrificial Program within a Cultural History of Sacrifice* (University Park: Pennsylvania State University Press, 1992), chapter 7, "The Sacrificial Program of Jesus."

36. Indeed, the reference to Zechariah (from "Q") is as securely attested as Jesus' reference to Isaiah (cf. Matt. 13:14; 15:7; Mark 7:6). The importance of

concerns the establishment of restored worship in the Temple, especially at the feast of Sukkoth (14:16–19). "All the nations" are to go up to Jerusalem annually for worship (v. 16), and the transformation of which that worship is part involves the provision of "living waters" from the city (v. 8, cf. John 4:10, 14). That image is related to an earlier "fountain opened for the house of David and the inhabitants of Jerusalem in view of sin and uncleanness" (13:1). Here we see the association of forgiveness and purity which is a feature of Jesus' program, as well as the notion of an immediate release, without any mention of sacrifice, from what keeps Israel from God. (There is, incidentally, also an indication of how the issue of Davidic ancestry might have featured in Jesus' ministry, quite aside from any messianic claim.)[37] God himself is held to arrange the purity he requires, so that the sacrifice he desires might take place.

Zechariah features the commissioning of a priest (chapter 3, cf. Matt. 16:18, 19),[38] an oracle against swearing (5:3, 4,[39] cf. 5:33–37), a vision of a king humbly riding an ass (9:9, cf. Matt. 21:1–9; Mark 11:1–10; Luke 19:28–40; John 12:12–19), and the prophetic receipt of thirty shekels of silver in witness against the owners of sheep (11:4–17, cf. Matt. 26:14–16; 27:3–10; Mark 14:10, 11; Luke 22:3–6). It is obvious that the connections between Jesus' ministry and Zechariah do not amount to a common agenda,

---

Zechariah in assessing Jesus' purpose has been stressed in Joachim Jeremias, *Jesus' Promise to the Nations*, trans. S. H. Hooke, Studies in Biblical Theology (London: SCM, 1958), 65–70; Cecil Roth, "The Cleansing of the Temple and Zechariah XIV 21," *Novum Testamentum* 4 (1960): 174–81. It is a commonplace of criticism to suggest that Matthew and Luke may originally have referred to Zechariah the priest in 2 Chronicles 24:20–22 (and cf. Zechariah, son of Baris, in *Jewish War* IV § 334–44), but the identification with the prophet, the son of Barachiah, is unambiguous in Matthew (and some witnesses to Luke). That the figure in mind is a product of haggadic embellishment, however, appears evident, and may draw upon the recollection of several people named "Zechariah."

37. See Bruce Chilton, "Jesus *ben David*: Reflections on the *Davidssohnfrage*," *Journal for the Study of the New Testament* 14 (1982): 88–112.

38. See Bruce Chilton, "Shebna, Eliakim, and the Promise to Peter," *Targumic Approaches to the Gospels: Studies in Judaism* (Lanham, Md.: University Press of America, 1986), 63–80, and *The Social World of Formative Christianity and Judaism*, ed. J. Neusner, P. Borgen, E. S. Frerichs, R. Horsley (Philadelphia: Fortress, 1989), 311–26.

39. Verse 3 refers simply to swearing, not to swearing deceitfully, as in v. 4, despite the impression given in the RSV.

and Matthew clearly reflects a tendency to increase the fit between the two. But the similarities may be suggestive of Jesus' appropriation of Zechariah's prophecy of eschatological purity, as a final, more fundamental connection would indicate. The climactic vision of Zechariah insists that every vessel in Jerusalem will belong to the LORD, and become a fit vessel for sacrifice. As part of that insistence, the text asserts that no trader will be allowed in the Temple (14:20, 21). In the light of Zechariah, Jesus' occupation of the Temple appears as an enactment of prophetic purity in the face of a commercial innovation,[40] a vigorous insistence that God would prepare his own people and vessels for eschatological worship.

Notably, the Targum of Zechariah specifically includes reference to God's kingdom at 14:9,[41] and that might represent another, programmatic link with Jesus. In any case, it is clear that Jesus understood the efficacy of sacrifice to derive from a purity and a forgiveness which God extended to Israel in anticipation of the climax of worship. In those understandings, Jesus was no doubt unusual in his immediate application of a prophetic program to the actual Temple, but far from unique. His precise demands concerning the provision of animals as offerings, however, show how the issue of purity was for him pragmatic, as well as affective. And it was in that Pharisaic vein[42] that he confronted the authorities in the Temple with the claim that their management was a scandal and that the direct provision of animals by a forgiven, purified Israel was what was required for the experience of holiness and the reality of the covenant to be achieved.

Whether or not Jesus' program was a precedent for Paul's, the mere existence of Zechariah, which Paul does at least allude to,[43] opens the possibility that Paul might have included an actual of-

---

40. See *The Temple of Jesus,* chapter 7, "Jesus' Occupation of the Temple."

41. See Kevin J. Cathcart and Robert P. Gordon, *The Targum of the Minor Prophets,* Aramaic Bible 14 (Wilmington: Glazier, 1989). As the editors indicate, the significance of the reference was earlier established in my article "Regnum Dei Deus Est," *Scottish Journal of Theology* 31 (1978): 261–70; cf. *Targumic Approaches to the Gospels,* 99–107.

42. As we have seen in volume 1 of our trilogy: chapter 5: "Jesus: The Genesis of Christian Interpretation."

43. See Romans 8:36; 1 Corinthians 2.11, 11:25; 13·5; 14:25.

fering from the gentiles in Jerusalem as a part of his program, and therefore as part of his meaning in Romans 15:16. The reading of the Targum of Zechariah is particularly pertinent at this point, quite aside from the question of its relationship to Jesus' preaching.

Over the past dozen years, a consensus has emerged regarding the dating of Targum Jonathan, a consensus which the Aramaic Bible series has both confirmed and helped to establish. In a work published in 1982, I suggested that the Targum of Isaiah should be understood to have developed in two principal stages, with the gathering and development of translations during the period between 70 C.E. and 135 C.E., and then again during the fourth century.[44] A version — perhaps incomplete — of Isaiah in Aramaic was composed by interpreters who flourished between 70 C.E. and 135 C.E.[45] That work was completed by other interpreters, associated with Rabbi Joseph bar Ḥiyya of Pumbeditha, who died in 333.[46] Throughout the process, however, the communal nature of the interpretative work of the interpreters is manifest; insofar as individuals were involved, they spoke as the voice of synagogues and of schools. My analysis of those phases as exegetical frameworks within the document, evidenced in characteristic theologoumena, has been confirmed in the cases of the Targums of the Former Prophets, of Jeremiah, Ezekiel, and the Minor Prophets.[47] The emphasis

---

44. See Bruce Chilton, *The Glory of Israel: The Theology and Provenience of the Isaiah Targum*, Journal for the Study of the Old Testament Supplements 23 (Sheffield: JSOT, 1982). It might be mentioned, in the interests of accuracy, that the date printed on the title page is an error. (Churgin's work suffered a similar fate, although the error involved misplacing his book by a decade! Cf. P. Churgin, *Targum Jonathan to the Prophets*, Yale Oriental Series [New Haven: Yale University Press, 1927].) In a condensed form, my conclusions are available in *The Isaiah Targum: Introduction, Translation, Apparatus, and Notes*, Aramaic Bible 11 (Wilmington: Glazier; Edinburgh: T. & T. Clark, 1987), xiii–xxx.

45. Within that early framework, materials were incorporated which appear to reflect the interpretations of earlier periods, including the period of Jesus; see Bruce Chilton, *A Galilean Rabbi and His Bible: Jesus' Use of the Interpreted Scripture of His Time*, Good News Studies 8 (Wilmington: Glazier, 1984); also published with the subtitle *Jesus' Own Interpretation of Isaiah* (London: SPCK, 1984).

46. Chilton, *The Glory of Israel*, 2, 3; *The Isaiah Targum*, xxi. For the sections of the Targum most representative of each stage of interpretation, see *The Isaiah Targum*, xxiv.

47. The model I developed for the Targum of Isaiah is applied in D. J.

within the fourteenth chapter of the Targum of Zechariah upon the inclusion of the nations in eschatological worship, and that within the Tannaitic framework (or phase) of the document, demonstrates that the motif which the Hebrew text and the Septuagint (see also Tobit 13:8–11) represent translated quite well within the concerns of the Aramaic interpreters.

Targum Jonathan, together with Tobit and sources such as Jubilees (see 4:26), establishes that the global range of the sanctuary was an expectation within early Judaism. Paul aimed, just as he said, to promote a literal offering of the nations by means of his collection for the needs of the church in Jerusalem. The book of Acts is at pains to exculpate Paul from the charge that he introduced gentiles into the precincts of the Temple (21:27–30), but precisely that accusation, mounted by Jews from Asia who were in a position to know what Paul intended (v. 27), is what in Acts produces the attempt to kill Paul and his subsequent (as it turned out, definitive) arrest (vv. 31f.). Acts may certainly not be consulted as a straightforwardly historical source, but the confused picture it conveys at this point may be said to be consistent with the finding from Paul's own letters that he intended that gentiles should be joined within the sacrificial worship of Israel.[48]

Because Paul conceives of Jews and non-Jews as being included as the seed of Abraham through Christ (see Gal. 3:29), they all have a place in the sacrificial worship of Israel. That vigorous assertion of inclusion requires a fresh understanding of how Jesus as the Son of Man and how the Spirit which is re-

---

Harrington and A. J. Saldarini, *Targum Jonathan of the Former Prophets*, Aramaic Bible 10 (Wilmington: Glazier; Edinburgh: T. & T. Clark, 1987), 3; Robert Hayward, *The Targum of Jeremiah*, Aramaic Bible 12 (Wilmington: Glazier; Edinburgh: T. & T. Clark, 1987), 38; S. H. Levey, *The Targum of Ezekiel*, Aramaic Bible 13 (Wilmington: Glazier; Edinburgh: T. & T. Clark, 1987), 3, 4; Cathcart and Gordon, *The Targum of the Minor Prophets*, 12–14. Levey's acceptance of the paradigm is especially noteworthy, in that he had earlier argued that Targum Jonathan (especially Isaiah) should be placed within the period of the ascendancy of Islam; cf. "The Date of Targum Jonathan to the Prophets," *Vetus Testamentum* 21 (1971): 186–96.

48. Particularly, the hypothesis explains why Paul, in Romans 9–11, is at pains to include all believers within the ambit of Israel at a moment of historic weakness in the Jewish community in Rome; see Bruce Chilton, "Romans 9–11 as Scriptural Interpretation and Dialogue with Judaism," *Ex Auditu* 4 (1988): 27–37.

leased by means of Jesus warrant the Pauline policy. Paul is not backward in providing the necessary redefinition.

He provides the key to his own thought in a characteristically direct way, within a discussion of the resurrection. Just as the first Adam became living being, Paul observes, so Jesus as the last Adam became life-giving Spirit (1 Cor. 15:45). The comparison between Christ and Adam occurred to Paul because the motif of the primordial human being was vital within early Judaism.[49] Paul's originality here can be appreciated only by comparing his conception to James's and to Peter's. Jesus is raised as the Son of Man here (unlike in James's thought), not as a special guarantor of the Temple as it stands, but as the heavenly Man who gives of Spirit to all who believe. They are then put in a position to bear his image and therefore to rise from the dead (see 1 Cor. 15:46–57). Similarly, Spirit here is not simply a matter of occasional revelation, as in the case of the Petrine mission to non-Jews, but becomes Paul's name for the ambience of Christian living which links faith now with the resurrection which is to come.

We have already seen in the previous chapter (pp. 114–117) that Paul's understanding of the Spirit of God in 1 Corinthians 15 is coordinated with his conception of the present operation of that same Spirit in 1 Corinthians 2. The dynamic of the Spirit in both cases is that of revealing and transforming. The resurrection of Jesus reveals a new Adam, and therefore a new humanity, such that people as they are experience the hope of what they shall be (1 Cor. 15). Similarly, by the power of the Spirit, God reveals the things he has prepared for those who love him, although such things are beyond their understanding in ordinary terms; that revelation makes for a spiritual teaching which can be received only by those who accept the Spirit bestowed by God rather than the spirit the world offers (1 Cor. 2).

The contrast Paul makes between the spirit of the world and the Spirit of God demonstrates clearly that, for him, human beings are spiritual (as well as psychic and fleshly) in at least one aspect of their existence. Paul does not claim that only those

---

49. See W. D. Davies, *Paul and Rabbinic Judaism* (London: SPCK, 1958), 36–57.

who are baptized are spiritual, but rather that the only appropriate content of that which longs for Spirit within us is the Spirit of God. The problem of the "spirit of the world" (1 Cor. 2:12) is simply that it is a false substitute for the proper counterpart of our desire to know God. Once Spirit has been received, it is possible for people to know God in God's own terms, which is Spirit, provided they do not confuse what God teaches with the wisdom of this world (1 Cor. 2:13).

That brings us to one of Paul's characteristic statements, a statement which can only seem perplexing if his anthropology is not kept in mind (1 Cor. 2:14):

> A psychic person does not receive the things of the Spirit of God, for they are foolishness to him and he is not able to know, because they are judged spiritually.

Here is the clearest possible assertion that the medium of faith for Paul is not soul (*psukhe*), but Spirit. And Spirit is such that it can become confused in regard to its proper aim. Because we live in a world with other people who seek spiritually, we are capable of manufacturing a purely human wisdom which comports with the spirit of this world. That is just what is disturbing the Christians in Corinth in Paul's analysis, which is why he goes to some lengths to distinguish the Spirit of God from what attempts to substitute for it. But the very danger of the substitution — indeed, the human predilection for it, in Paul's analysis — shows that the desire and the capacity for Spirit is intrinsically human. In fact, it is precisely the desire and the capacity for Spirit which brings with it the danger of confusion.

In contrast to the spirit of this world and the limitation to soul, Paul makes a startling claim about possession of the Spirit (1 Cor. 2:15–16):

> But the spiritual person judges all things, and is himself judged by no one. For who knows the mind of the Lord, that will instruct him? But we have the mind of Christ.

Two related thoughts are insistently expressed here. First, just as the spirit of the world is a poor substitute for the Spirit of God, so the world is in no position to understand or judge someone

who has received the Spirit. The incomprehension, even the en-
mity, of those around one who has been baptized, if they are
also not of the Church, is to be anticipated, and even accepted as
inevitable. Second, the exact medium by which the Spirit of God
is known by us spiritually is, in the light of baptism, identifi-
able. That medium is the mind of Christ, the person in imitation
of whom one enters the water and emerges with a fresh identity,
as a child of God.

Summary

"The Son of Man" and "the Spirit of God" relate God, Jesus,
and the believer throughout the circles of Christianity which
have been discussed. But there is a characteristic spirituality in
each case. For James, Jesus is the Son of Man enthroned on high,
and the Temple is the closest point of proximity to him on earth.
Within the circle of Peter, Jesus is the point of access for God's
own Spirit, and God may choose through this revelation to alter
what he said through Moses. In the case of Stephen's vision, the
principle of alteration becomes revolutionary and involves making the Son of Man the antithesis of the Temple itself. Paul's
position is in fact less radical, in that there is still a place for
the Temple, but here the emphasis on communion with God
through the Spirit leaves no room for any other truly regulative
principle of prayer.

Within these circles and others like them, what we know
as the Lord's Prayer would have been known and used. Jesus'
spirituality of the kingdom was never forgotten. But the understanding of how such prayer through the risen Jesus was
possible became distinctive in such groups as they developed
their own views of authority (see volume 1 of the trilogy)
and their own conceptions of community within distinct social
settings (see volume 2 of the trilogy). A truly ecumenical christology did not yet exist, and the need for such an instrument to
allay tensions within the movement as a whole was obvious.

Epilogue

Son of God, Incarnation

The Synoptic Son of God

Consensus within primitive Christianity included agreement that prayer should be in the manner of Jesus. His mastery of invoking the kingdom was passed on to his disciples and became a characteristic part of Christian practice, as we considered in chapter 4. At the same time, the Christian consensus held that Jesus himself, after his resurrection, warranted and enabled such prayer. He might be held to do so as the Son of Man accessible within the worship in the Temple (so the circle of James), as the bestower of Spirit in the manner of Moses (so the circle of Peter), as the Son of Man who stood against worship in the Temple (so the position of Stephen), or as a new Adam who puts us in a new relationship to the Spirit of God (so Paul). That variety has taken up our attention in chapter 5. Now we consider how that variety was coordinated within the Synoptic Gospels, so as to provide an ecumenical consensus for early Christianity.

The role of the Synoptic Gospels in the foundation of consensus within the catechesis of the Church has already been discussed in our trilogy.[1] The written forms of the first three Gospels were produced after the destruction of the Temple, Mark in Rome (c. 71 C.E.), Matthew in Damascus (c. 80 C.E.), and Luke in Antioch (c. 90 C.E.). But they all rely upon a common and widely disseminated paradigm for the preparation of candidates for baptism. That common paradigm is most plau-

---

1. See volume 1 of our trilogy: chapter 6, "The Interpretative Resolution of the New Testament"; and volume 2: chapter 7, "The Synoptic Gospels, Paul, Hebrews, and the Revelation: Practicing the Body of Christ."

sibly associated with the ministry of Barnabas in Antioch and emerged around the year 50 C.E. Its presentation of Jesus conveys a definitive understanding of how the believer knows God through Christ and how the believer is transformed by that knowledge.

Because "the kingdom of God" is particularly associated with Jesus in the Synoptic Gospels, the phrase does not simply refer to a topic within the religious language of Judaism. There is a commonly Synoptic *transformation* of the usual meaning of the kingdom within Judaism, such that Jesus alone discloses the kingdom.[2] The Synoptic transformation of the kingdom essentially involves a unique pattern of the distribution of sayings and of their narrative context within Jesus' ministry. The result is to focus upon Jesus as the herald who alone preaches the kingdom, the advocate who alone explains the kingdom, and the guarantor whose death attests to the reality of the kingdom. The transformation is sufficiently general so that how each Synoptic Gospel construes the meaning of the kingdom as conveyed by Jesus may be described as a variation on a theme.

The last phase of the Synoptic transformation of the kingdom is especially telling. It pursues the logic of the identification of Jesus and the kingdom to its final point: Jesus' death and the kingdom are presented as mutually explicating. "I shall not drink of the fruit of the vine again, until I drink it with you new in God's kingdom" (see Matt. 26:29; Mark 14:25; Luke 22:18). Within the Synoptics, the saying serves to insist that the same Jesus who announced and taught the kingdom is also, by means of his death and resurrection, the sole guarantor of its glorious coming (cf. the similar function of Luke 22:29, 30; 23:42). The notices regarding Jesus' burial in Mark (15:43) and Luke (23:51) — that Joseph of Arimathea was one of those who anticipated the kingdom — serve to underscore just this feature of the Synoptic transformation.

The narrative of Jesus' passion is commonly agreed to constitute one of the earliest layers of the Synoptic tradition. Paul, for example, speaks of his preaching of the crucifixion in the

---

2. The specifics of the transformation have already been discussed in volume 1 of our trilogy, chapter 6.

letter to the Galatians c. 53 C.E. (see Gal. 3:1).[3] Because Mark's Gospel (as compared to the other two Synoptics) emphasizes events more than particular instances of Jesus' teaching, its presentation of the significance of the crucifixion is especially stark. The hearer or reader has attention focused on the fact of Jesus' teaching, more than on what he teaches, because the issue of recognizing Jesus, for who he truly is, is paramount here. That Jesus is the messiah, God's Son, is stated openly from the outset (1:1) and is confirmed supernaturally, by voices both divine (1:11; 9:7) and demonic (1:24, 34; 3:11; 5:7), and yet is missed by Jesus' contemporaries generally (1:27) and even the disciples (4:41). Peter's confession at Caesarea Philippi is accurate in its wording as far as it goes (8:29), and yet it proves to be substantively wrong (vv. 32b–33). At the end of the day, only an anonymous centurion, in the midst of Jesus' suffering, can voice the truth about Jesus in human terms and confess that Jesus is God's Son (15:39).

The issue of Mark, it seems clear, is not that there is any "messianic secret," as has often been claimed in the history of scholarship. There is no lack of clarity regarding the identity of Jesus. The ambiguity is only the hearer's or reader's, as he or she comes to decide whether to side with the centurion or with the high priest, who is told Jesus' identity openly and does not believe (14:61–64). The Markan Jesus, as in 14:61–62, says what must be said, and yet prefers silence; silence is, in the conditions presumed in this Gospel, a natural feature of that discipleship which understands who Jesus is (16:8). The wisdom of silence is that speaking of Jesus will bring persecution; Mark's Gospel was written after the vicious persecution under Nero in 64 C.E. The knowledge of silence in Mark concerns the Son of God.

The moment at which Jesus is most fully disclosed as God's Son in Mark is when he is crucified. Then the centurion sees his death and knows with whom he has been dealing (Mark 15:39). The phrase "God's Son" stems from the tradition of Hebrew Wisdom, which was readily accessible in Greek. The Wisdom of Solomon, a work of the first century B.C.E. composed in Greek,

---

3. For a study of the Passion Narrative, see Raymond E. Brown, *The Death of the Messiah* (New York: Doubleday, 1994).

speaks of a persecuted, righteous man as God's Son (see Wisd. 2:18).[4] Here the point of the usage is God's relationship to Jesus by means of vindication. Earlier, in the sayings of Jesus, sonship implied relationship by means of revelation: the Father revealed all to the Son (see Matt. 11:27; Luke 10:22, discussed in the last chapter).

The reason for the emphasis accorded to the centurion's confession becomes plain when we consider the narrative structure of the Synoptic Gospels generally. In aggregate, they initially highlight baptism, a single moment of communion which is both public and private. They address that moment by relating the baptism of Jesus at the hands of John the Baptist (Matt. 3:13–17; Mark 1:9–11; Luke 3:21–22). Here Jesus is addressed unequivocally by God as "my son," and from that point the Spirit which descends upon him governs his actions. The emphasis upon the latter motif is such that Jesus, after the baptism, is portrayed as being brought by the Spirit into the wilderness for his temptation (Matt. 4:1; Mark 1:12; Luke 4:1). His baptism commences the public ministry and the spiritual dynamism of Jesus.

The claims made for Jesus' baptism are all the more dramatic against the background of what may be surmised of the ministry of John the Baptist. According to Josephus, John practiced ablutions and preached righteousness in the wilderness (*Antiquities* 18 §§ 116–19). John's practice of generic baptism, dipping people in water so that they might become pure in their commitment to righteous repentance, seems quite distinct from the experience of Jesus as conveyed by the Synoptics. By the time the first three Gospels were composed, baptism had been appropriated within Jesus' movement.

In a passage already considered and commonly regarded as a reflection of a truly evangelical oral tradition, Peter in the book of Acts preaches in the house of the Roman centurion Cornelius and begins the gospel of Jesus with reference to the baptism preached by John (Acts 10:37–38). The result of his preaching is that the Holy Spirit falls upon those present (v. 44), and Peter

---

4. Indeed, Luke simply has the centurion speak of Jesus as "just" (see Luke 23:47), although Matthew (27:54) agrees with the presentation of Mark.

proceeds to baptize them with water (vv. 46c–48). Peter is here portrayed as authorizing the baptism of gentiles, despite the astonishment of his companions, who are "of the circumcision" (v. 45). The Synoptic Gospels are telling the story of Jesus' baptism for people who themselves could be baptized because the movement's membership was no longer exclusively Jewish. The content of baptism had been changed: it was now baptism "in the name of Jesus Christ" (v. 48, a formulation found frequently in Acts).

The notion of baptism into Jesus' name represents a transformation of John's program of ritual and ethical purification. It is impossible, on the face of the texts of the Synoptic Gospels, to determine what "happened" to Jesus in baptism, as distinct from what happened in the practice of predominantly gentile Christians. That indeterminacy between what occurred in the past and what is appropriated in the present is enshrined within the texts themselves. At the crucial moment, when it concerns the experience of being baptized, the Synoptic Gospels present interesting (and distinctive) qualifications:

Matthew 3:16
Having been baptized, immediately Jesus arose from the water; and lo, the heavens were opened, and he saw God's Spirit descending as a dove, coming upon him

Mark 1:9c–10
...and he was baptized in the Jordan by John. And immediately, arising from the water, he saw the heavens split, and the spirit as a dove descending upon him

Luke 3:21b–22
...and Jesus having been baptized, while he was praying, heaven was opened, and the Holy Spirit descended in bodily form as a dove upon him.

Although the Synoptic Gospels are comparable here, there is no question of a verbatim identity among them.

Nonetheless, each presents the baptism as a function of Jesus' own experience, as well as of what was said and done. In Matthew, the statement is made that the heavens were opened, but then the descent of the Spirit is described as what Jesus — and, apparently, Jesus alone — saw. Mark's wording presents both the heavenly tear[5] and the descent of the dove of the Spirit as matters of what only Jesus could have attested. Luke's language might seem to refer to objective events, but what is related is cast as a matter of what transpired while Jesus was praying after his baptism.

What is the reason for such frustrating indeterminacy? Why not merely state what happened and say what it means? Scholars of the New Testament commonly appeal to what are taken to be the looser standards of ancient historiography, but such explanations are superficial. The catechumen who was prepared for full admission into the society of Christians in Damascus (by Matthew) or Rome (by Mark) or Antioch (by Luke) was to be baptized into Jesus Christ's name and therefore to receive the Spirit of God. The narrative of Jesus' baptism was naturally presented as a paradigm of what the catechumen was to experience. The voice which addresses Jesus as the divine son, in whom God is well pleased (Matt. 3:17/Mark 1:11/Luke 3:22b), is saying what Jesus, God, and the Church know, but what Jesus' contemporaries are said not to have grasped. The Gospels deliberately speak out of time in order to convey their timely knowledge to the catechumen.

The indeterminacy between what might be said of Jesus and what may be said by the follower at baptism is, then, no quirk of the Synoptic Gospels, nor a matter of literary presentation alone. This is not just an unfortunate confusion, but a systemic feature of Christianity: the narrative identification in baptism between the believer and Jesus Christ. What happens to Jesus in baptism happens to him as God's Son, and when one joins the centurion in recognizing him as such, the way is open to baptism. The centurion at the foot of the cross keeps the place of Cornelius and of any subsequent hearer or reader of the gospel of Jesus.

Within the Synoptic Gospels, Jesus as the Son of God is both the object and the vehicle of divine revelation. His status as the place where God and humanity meet is consistent with the ear-

---

5. The same verb which will refer to the tear in the veil of the Temple after Jesus' crucifixion in Mark 15:38.

lier christologies of James and Peter and Stephen (and with the contemporaneous christology of Paul). At the same time, "Son of God" will put all the other christologies in its shadow, for two reasons. First, its immediate reference to God accords it logical priority over any other title. Second, the way the phrase is inextricably bound up with the passion of Jesus provides it with an emotional resonance second to no other designation.

Yet the prominence of the Son of God as the appropriate designation of Jesus has, in the history of the Church, often resulted in an ignorance of one vital aspect of its meaning. Because Jesus is baptized as God's Son, baptism in his name bestows the Spirit of his sonship upon the believer. Incarnation, in other words, is both a task of discipleship and a description of Jesus' peculiar role. Becoming God is something to do as well as something to rejoice in.

The Task of Incarnation

The last novel of Fyodor Dostoyevsky, *The Brothers Karamozov*, represents the culmination of the great novelist's effort (throughout his career) to depict fully a human character as Christ-like.[6] His greatest success comes in his development of the character of Alyosha, the third of the brothers.

Alyosha becomes devoted to a priest and monk named Zossima. The fame of Father Zossima is such that a miracle is expected at the time of his death. Instead, a scandal boils up because the smell of decay comes unexpectedly from Zossima's corpse. The contrast was unmistakable with pious legends about the bodies of saintly monks which were said never to decompose. The whole incident is vividly recounted in the context of the jealousies and false expectations of human communities. Dostoyevsky calls the entire chapter "The Odour of Corruption." It is the opening of Book Seven, called "Alyosha."[7]

---

6. The novel was completed in 1880; see the Penguin edition, trans. D. Magarshack (Harmondsworth: Penguin, 1985). The theme of the author's preoccupation with the figure of Christ is taken up in Konstantin Mochulsky, *Dostoevsky: His Life and Work*, trans. M. A. Minihan (Princeton: Princeton University Press, 1967).

7. That is also the start of part 3 of the four-part novel as a whole

Alyosha's reaction to the events is to leave the hermitage in great confusion. The opportunity is taken by a malicious acquaintance to lure Alyosha into a night of decadence. (One sort of corruption encourages another.) His attitude is summed up by his sneering remark to Alyosha at the close of the evening, "But you're not Christ, you know, and I'm not Judas."[8] There is no inadvertence in Dostoyevsky's writing here, because he is about to begin the transformation of Alyosha into a Christ in the next chapter.

Alyosha returns to the hermitage, to the cell which holds Zossima's corpse. Another priest is reading the story of the wedding at Cana in Galilee, from John's Gospel (John 2:1–11[9]) when Jesus provides wine for the company. Just as the moment in the Gospel comes when the steward of the feast says, "You have kept the good wine until now," Alyosha has a vision. He is at the wedding with the guests, and Zossima is there as well. Zossima even offers a vision of Christ, "Do you see our Sun, do you see him?" When Alyosha expresses fear, Zossima goes on:

> Do not be afraid of him. He's terrible in his majesty, awful in his eminence, but infinitely merciful. He became like one of us from love and he makes merry with us, turns water into wine, so as not to cut short the gladness of the guests. He is expecting new guests, he is calling new ones unceasingly and for ever and ever.

The ecstasy of the encounter is underlined, but so is its purely visionary character, because it ends when Alyosha wakes up.

Dostoyevsky goes on, however, to craft the scene in the light of his own insight concerning where divine empowerment occurs. Alyosha rushes out of the cell and falls onto the earth under the stars. Not in the cell of vision, but here, in the world of nature and in his awareness of other people, Alyosha has the experience which will transform his life:

---

8. At the end of chapter 3.

9. Another reading from John, the story of the raising of Lazarus (John 11:1–45), is the pivotal moment in an earlier novel, *Crime and Punishment*. The narrative technique is essentially the same within both works, in the interweaving of the reading with the characters' thoughts, although Dostoyevsky's writing in this regard was more accomplished by the time he came to write *Karamozov*.

He wanted to forgive everyone and for everything, and to beg forgiveness...for all and for everything.... It echoed in his soul again. But with every moment he felt clearly and almost palpably that something firm and immovable, like the firmament itself, was entering his soul. A sort of idea was gaining an ascendancy over his mind — and that for the rest of his life, for ever and ever. He had fallen upon the earth a weak youth, but he rose from it a resolute fighter for the rest of his life, and he realized it and felt it suddenly, at the very moment of his rapture.

With unfailing accuracy, Dostoyevsky here identifies the precise dynamic which is at work in Christian faith. Vision is only the prelude; what follows is forgiveness and the inspiring resolution (that is, the strength of spirit) which follows.

Dostoyevsky has Father Zossima say to Alyosha during the vision, "Begin your work, my dear one, begin your work, my gentle one!" The scene is baptismal in everything but setting, and it incorporates the great themes of baptism: vision, forgiveness, empowerment by means of Spirit. In his depiction of Alyosha, Dostoyevsky approached his ideal, as expressed in his appreciation of the Gospel according to John: "it finds the whole miracle in the *incarnation* alone, in the manifestation of the beautiful alone."[10] The realization of that miracle, within the terms of conditions in Russia, was also the aim of Dostoyevsky's work.

What Dostoyevsky laid bare was what is implicit in the Gospels, the twofold meaning of the Incarnation. Incarnation first concerns Jesus, as that place where the divine and the human meet. He is the Son of Man, the source of Spirit in the manner of Moses, and the final Adam, all because he is God's Son. As God's Son, his vision may become ours. He teaches us to see the kingdom as he does, and in so doing becomes a vision for us. That is when the Incarnation concerns us, directly as forgiveness reconciles us to this Son of God, and the force of the resulting power transforms our lives.

---

10. Mochulsky, *Dostoevsky*, 345, citing a letter to Dostoyevsky's niece, S. A. Ivanova.

Index of
Ancient Sources

General Index

174